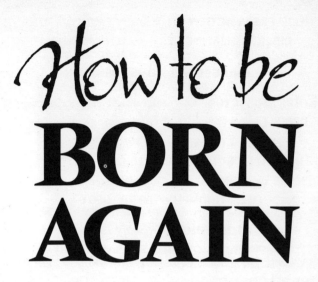

# How to be
# BORN
# AGAIN

# T.L. OSBORN
### Introduction by Dr. LaDonna Osborn

# BOOKS BY THE OSBORNS

**BELIEVERS IN ACTION**—*Apostolic–Rejuvenating*

**BIBLICAL HEALING**—*Seven Miracle-Keys*
*4 Visions–50+ yrs. of Proof–324 Merged Bible Vs.*

**FIVE CHOICES FOR WOMEN WHO WIN**
*21st Century Options*

**GOD'S BIG PICTURE**—*An Impelling Gospel Classic*

**GOD'S LOVE PLAN**—*The Awesome Discovery*

**HEALING THE SICK**—*A Living Classic*

**HOW TO BE BORN AGAIN**—*The Miracle-Book*

**JESUS and WOMEN**—*Big Questions Answered*

**LIFE—TRIUMPH OVER TRAGEDY**
*A True Story of Life After Death*

**NEW LIFE FOR WOMEN**—*Reality Refocused*

**SOULWINNING–OUTSIDE THE SANCTUARY**
*A Classic on Biblical Christianity & Human Dignity*

**THE BEST OF LIFE**—*Seven Energizing Dynamics*

**THE GOOD LIFE**—*A Mini-Bible School–1,467 Ref.*

**THE GOSPEL ACCORDING TO T.L. & DAISY**
*Their Life & World Ministry–510 pg. Pictorial*

**THE MESSAGE THAT WORKS**
*T.L.'s Revealing Manifesto on Biblical Faith*

**THE POWER OF POSITIVE DESIRE**
*An Invigorating Faith Perspective*

**THE WINNING SECRET**
*Biblical Refocus of Spiritual Warfare*

**THE WOMAN BELIEVER**
*Awareness of God's Design*

**WOMAN WITHOUT LIMITS**
*Unmuzzled—Unfettered—Unimpeded*

**WOMEN & SELF-ESTEEM**
*Divine Royalty Unrestrained*

**YOU ARE GOD'S BEST**
*Transforming Life-Discoveries*

**OSBORN**
PUBLISHERS

---

*OSBORN INTERNATIONAL*
T.L. OSBORN, FOUNDER & PRES.
LADONNA OSBORN, V.P. & CEO

P.O. Box 10, Tulsa, OK 74102 USA

Tel: 918/743-6231
Fax: 918/749-0339   E-Mail: OSFO@aol.com
www.OSBORN.ORG

---

**Canada:** Box 281, Adelaide St. Post Sta., Toronto  M5C 2J4
**England:** Box 148, Birmingham  B3 2LG
(A Registered Charity)

BIBLE QUOTATIONS IN THIS BOOK MAY BE PER-
SONALIZED, PARAPHRASED, ABRIDGED OR CONFORMED
TO THE *PERSON* AND *TENSE* OF THEIR CONTEXTUAL AP-
PLICATION, TO FOSTER CLARITY AND INDIVIDUAL AC-
CEPTANCE. VARIOUS LANGUAGES AND VERSIONS HAVE
BEEN CONSIDERED. CHAPTER AND VERSE REFERENCES EN-
ABLE THE READER TO COMPARE THE PASSAGES WITH HIS
OR HER OWN BIBLE. (SEE PAGE 200 FOR ABBREVIA-
TIONS OF BIBLE BOOKS USED IN THIS WORK.)

THE AUTHOR

ISBN 0-87943-131-8
Copyright 2002 by LaDonna C. Osborn
Printed in the United States of America
All Rights Reserved

# Contents

|   | Introduction | 9 |
|---|---|---|
|   | Foreword | 11 |
| 1 | Miracle Rebirth | 17 |
| 2 | The Buddhist Nun | 21 |
| 3 | The Reborn Prostitute | 31 |
| 4 | Understanding The New Birth | 43 |
| 5 | Become A Child of God | 47 |
| 6 | Revelation of Divine *Love* | 51 |
| 7 | Killer Pardoned | 61 |
| 8 | Ricardo, I Am Jesus! | 69 |
| 9 | The Moslem Trader | 75 |
| 10 | The Insane Beggar | 83 |
| 11 | Of This, You Can Be Sure | 93 |
| 12 | The Mystery Revealed | 97 |
| 13 | The Abyss That Separates | 103 |
| 14 | New Perspective | 111 |
| 15 | Embracing Truth | 119 |
| 16 | The Greatest Miracle | 125 |
| 17 | Transformation | 137 |
| 18 | Biblical Faith | 143 |
| 19 | Now You are Born Again | 163 |
| 20 | New *Life*style | 175 |
| 21 | Decision On Record | 178 |
| 22 | The Good *Life* is for YOU | 181 |
| 23 | Promises To Treasure | 183 |
| 24 | Finding the Answer | 189 |
| 25 | A Daily Prayer | 191 |
| 26 | The Love Letter | 195 |
|   | Bible-Book Abbreviations | 200 |
|   | OSBORN Global Ministry | 201 |

# DEDICATION

I DEDICATE THIS book to every person regardless of race, sex, nationality or religious background who feels a sense of fear, condemnation or insecurity about death and the hereafter and who would like to know that he or she can come to God in simple faith, receive eternal forgiveness and be BORN AGAIN by His divine power, becoming a child of God with all of the privileges of His Royal Family and of His Abundant Living.

The Author

# INTRODUCTION

**M**ANY BOOKS have been written *about* human spirituality, attempting to answer the questions that are embedded within the human psyche. Reading them, one often feels like an eavesdropper, overhearing an analytical discussion about one's needs and goals.

This book is different. As you read HOW TO BE BORN AGAIN, you will feel as though my father, the author, is seated beside you, responding to your questions and to your deepest needs. This book is not written *about* you. It is written *to* you.

The truths that you will discover between these covers can transform your thinking and your living forever!

Religious arguments do not bring peace.

Ideological comparisons do not result in answers to one's needs.

Empty worship rituals do not ease a person's guilt.

Attempts to act right do not change the human heart.

But there is a valid way to find peace with God, to solve life's tough problems, to answer the deepest questions, to exchange guilt for genuine forgiveness, inferiority for dignity, insignificance for new personhood — to experience a total change of heart and to discover a new beginning.

Dr. T.L. Osborn has written this book to guide you into a new and vibrant way of living. He has invested his entire life helping people in nearly 100 nations to discover how much God loves them and how they can respond to His *Life*-transforming, *Love*-healing power.

Being involved in our world ministry from childhood, I have seen tens of thousands of lives transformed by the miraculous energy of God's *Love*. Some of their stories are being shared with you in this book as proof that no person is hopeless or beyond the reach of God's *Love*.

You too will discover how your life can be regenerated and how you can have a new beginning. Wouldn't it be wonderful to find out that it is not too late for a new start? That is the Good News. You too can be BORN AGAIN.

—LaDonna C. Osborn, D.Min.

# FOREWORD

A CHILD AT THE age of three was asked: "What do you want to be when you grow up?" Without hesitation, he replied: "I want to be a chimpanzee and sit up in a tree and eat bananas."

Three years later, that child was asked the same question. He replied: "I want to be a spaceman, and find out what is out there."

In just three years, that boy's self-image evolved from being a chimpanzee to becoming a spaceman—which depicts how rapidly people can change.

An old axiom says, "Human nature never changes." But that is not true. Every*thing* and every*one* IS changing all the time, for better or for worse. A nice plot of soil can become a beautiful garden, or if left to its own, will become an ugly patch of weeds.

There was a beautiful statue of Diana atop New York's old Madison Square Garden. A lovely young woman posed for the statue and became famous. But then her life deteriorated and she become dissolute. Years later, a battered old woman stumbled into the Salvation Army kitchen, begging for bread and soup. When the officer asked her name, he gasped, "Then *you* are Diana." A twisted smile came across her wretched face as she replied, "I *was* Diana."

Millions live with a sense of failure and futility, of defeat and disaster, of conflict and division, of fears and resentments, of inferiorities, of self-loathing, of boredom and of guilt. These processes distort minds and destroy lives. People search for answers and live in skepticism. If life is to be beautiful as God planned it, the answer to human dilemmas is to be BORN AGAIN.

The simple concepts in this book can plant in you the seeds of divine *Life* – goodness, happiness, dignity, productivity, health, integrity, peace. Divine *Life* is supernatural *Life* – God's *Life* that He intended for all who believe in Him to experience.

I've written this book to guide you toward a fresh, new beginning. While you read these pages, the seeds of divine *Life* will be planted in the garden of your life. If you believe these basic biblical truths, they will generate a harvest of God's kind of *Life* in you. Don't *try* to make the seeds grow and produce a harvest. Just read, and believe. God will do the miracle.

This book is not a thesis, a theory or a treatise about God or religion. It is a guide toward a fresh horizon of a new lifestyle where peace and achievement, joy and health, blessing and fulfillment will flourish in your life.

In religion, almost every voice tells unconverted people that they are worthless, unholy and doomed to destruction. I've shared Christ with millions, face to face, and I have witnessed villages, cities and even nations changed or greatly influenced by the biblical message of Good News. But I have never harangued the unconverted, or condemned them.

God's true message is that you are valuable; that your life has infinite purpose; that He has paid to redeem you and to draw you to His side as a partner; that you are indispensable to His divine plan; that He believes in you and that He loves you *just as you are*; that He offers you a total new beginning.

If your life has been a zero, or if it has failed to match your dreams, this book will show you how to identify with God, how to believe in His *Love* and how to embrace the truths that will regenerate and enhance your life and your thinking.

You will forget how you thought before you understood these ideas about God. Your new rapport and friendship with Him will produce new positivism and purpose in life.

As you read, the process of transformation will take place. Step by step, you will discover reasons for peace, the why of faith, the delight of discovery, the resolve to think new, the process of believing, the energy of new truth. You will find yourself embracing the transforming power of a **new kind of *Life*** and the miraculous dignity of a **new kind of *Love***.

Friendship with God who believes in you, will replace condemnation, guilt and inferiority. Rapport with God who trusts you and loves you, will lead you to the joy of camaraderie with Him. Intimacy with God who ransomed you will introduce you to a dynamic new lifestyle — not of religion but of refreshing veracity in your spiritual relationship as His child and as a *bona-fide* member of His Royal Family.

Remember, the divine *Seed of Truth* will do its work in the soil of your heart. Just plant it (by reading these truths), and you will discover the mystery of *Christ in you* Col.1:27 and the miracle of being BORN AGAIN.

—T.L. OSBORN

WHOEVER believes the Gospel of Christ and receives Him in their lives by faith, is BORN AGAIN— not a physical rebirth by human procreation, but a *rebirth* of the human spirit by divine procreation— a Miracle.

The apostle John said, *As many as received Him, to them He gave power to become the sons* [and the daughters] *of God.* Joh.1:12

John explains that they are BORN AGAIN, *not of blood, nor of the will of the flesh, nor of the will of man, but of God.*Joh. 1:12-13

16

# CHAPTER 1

# Miracle Rebirth

## ST. JOHN 1: LIVING BIBLE

*B*EFORE ANYTHING *else existed, there was Christ, with God. He has always been alive and is Himself God.*[v.1]

*He created everything there is — nothing exists that He did not make.*[v.3]

*Eternal life is in Him and this Life gives light to all of humankind.*[v.4]

*His Life is the light that shines through the darkness — and the darkness can never extinguish it.*[v.5]

*But although He made the world, the world didn't recognize Him when He came. Even in His own land and among His own people…He was not accepted. Only a few would welcome and receive Him. But to all who received Him, He gave the right to become children of God. All they needed to do was to trust Him to save them.*[vs.10-12]

*All those who believe this are **reborn**! — not a physical **rebirth** resulting from human passion or plan — but from the Will of God.*[v.13]

## ST. JOHN 3: LIVING BIBLE

*A*FTER DARK *one night a Jewish religious leader named Nicodemus, a member of the sect of the Pharisees, came for an interview with Jesus. 'Sir,' he said, 'we all know that God has sent You to teach us. Your miracles are proof enough of this.'*[vs.1-2]

*Jesus replied, 'With all the earnestness I possess I tell you this: Unless you are* BORN AGAIN *you can never get into the Kingdom of God.'*[v.3]

*'BORN AGAIN!' exclaimed Nicodemus. 'What do You mean? How can an old man go back into his mother's womb and be* BORN AGAIN*?'*[v.4]

*Jesus replied, 'What I am telling you so earnestly is this: Unless one is born of water and the Spirit, he* [or she] *cannot enter the Kingdom of God.*[v.5]

*'Men can only reproduce human life, but the Holy Spirit gives new Life from heaven;*[v.6]

*'So don't be surprised at my statement that you must be* BORN AGAIN*!'*[v.7]

*As MOSES in the wilderness lifted up the bronze image of a serpent on a pole,*[Num.21:7-9] *even so I must be lifted upon a pole [the cross], so that anyone who believes in me will have eternal Life.*[vs.14-15]

*For God loved the world so much that He gave His only Son so that anyone who believes in Him shall not perish but have eternal Life.*[v.16]

*God did not send His Son into the world to condemn it, but to save it.*[v.17]

*There is no eternal doom awaiting those who trust Him to save them.*[v.18]

I CAN TELL YOU that people are basically the same worldwide. They commit the same sins, experience the same needs, sense the same guilt, suffer the same diseases and instinctively search for the same peace, regardless of race, sex, color, nationality or background.

# CHAPTER 2

# The Buddhist Nun

**F**OR NEARLY sixty years we have proclaimed the Gospel of Christ in almost one hundred nations of the world.

We always conduct our crusades out on open fields or in parks, stadiums or public grounds, so that the people of all religions and of all social and racial backgrounds can attend freely.

During nearly six decades, we have talked about the *new birth* before audiences of from 15,000 to 300,000 people nightly. In this book I am sharing the same truths that we have shared with literally millions of people worldwide. I have tried to write these things just as if you and I were having a private *tête-à-tête*.

This is a book that WORKS LIKE A MIRACLE. If you just read it through, with your heart open and sincere, and if you desire the peace that comes with a right relationship with God, then you can be soundly converted before you have finished these pages.

I have watched thousands of Moslems, Buddhists, Shintoists, Hindus, fetish-worshipers, atheists and nominal Christians discover Jesus Christ, receive Him into their hearts and become radiant new creatures when they came to understand the simple but powerful facts you will discover in this book.

Perhaps no couple on earth has proclaimed the Gospel to so many multitudes of so many different religious backgrounds as my wife and I have been privileged to do during our decades of ministry together.

From our global experience, I can tell you that people are basically the same worldwide. They commit the same sins, experience the same needs, sense the same guilt, suffer the same diseases and instinctively search for the same peace, regardless of race, sex, color, nationality or background.

✧✧✧

WHEN ANYONE is really BORN AGAIN, he or she discovers overwhelming spiritual satisfaction and real *peace with God*. I have watched thousands of stoic and traditionally imperturbable American Indians, Eskimos, Japanese and Thai people experience the miracle of the *new birth*. The effect upon their lives is no different than what happened to people in Bible days.

Thousands of Moslems have decided to believe on Christ during our gospel crusades and have experienced the *new birth*, with the same reactions and results being witnessed in their lives as one might expect in the people in Texas, Togo, Trinidad or Taiwan.

As this edition of this book goes to press, I have just returned from some enormous crusades in three nations of *Afrique Francophone*. In one meeting, an extended family of twenty Moslems came to the platform to publicly confess that they had been BORN AGAIN, committing themselves to follow Christ. In another meeting, seven Moslems did the same.

We have watched placid and imperturbable Buddhists break into tears of gratitude as they became believers in Jesus Christ and were BORN AGAIN.

We have proven what Paul said: *For there is no difference…the same Lord over all is rich unto all that call upon Him, for **whoever** shall call upon the Name of the Lord shall be saved.* Rom.10:12-13

◇◇◇

**D**URING ONE OF our crusades in Thailand, a 74 year old Buddhist nun was BORN AGAIN. She was placed in the Buddhist temple when she was a girl and had lived her life serving the priests and the temple.

Our crusade was conducted amidst a huge coconut palm grove where the sound from our loud speakers reached her ears. What she heard deeply affected her and she decided to attend.

Since her only clothing was a nun's habit, she slipped away from the temple to secretly buy a piece of cloth at the market with which she could conceal her identity as a Buddhist nun.

She stood at the edge of the field to avoid recognition.

That night I spoke about the *new birth* and the Good News of what Jesus accomplished on the Cross for all people. I announced the Scriptures about how humankind had sinned against God and was lost; how God loved those whom He had created so much that He gave His Son to bare the guilt and to suffer the judgment that humanity deserved, and how He shed His blood to purge us from our sins; that He died in our place, was buried and then rose from the dead, and that He sits at the right hand of God to intercede for us; that He is now knocking at the door of each heart wanting to impart His *Life*, peace, forgiveness, health and blessing to whoever believes on Him and receives Him.

I explained that sin is what separates humanity from God and causes guilt and fear; that since Jesus Christ suffered the judgment of our sins, if we will *only believe* that He did that for us personally, we will be *saved*; that since our sins have been *purged*, Heb.1:3 they can no longer separate us from Christ and therefore, He can come into our lives; and when that happens, one is *reborn* and becomes a new creation.

Standing amidst that multitude of Buddhists, under that huge coconut grove, that was the first time for that nun to hear the Good News about Jesus Christ.

When she came up on the platform to confess Christ publicly, we asked if she might come, the next day, to the little house where we were living to tell us more about her experience.

She came and for two hours we sat out under beautiful palm trees while that converted nun told us, through the interpreter, what had happened in her life.

Her eyes glittered like a young maiden as she expressed how she had received Jesus Christ and had been BORN AGAIN.

She said "All of my life, I searched for peace. The only thing I knew to do was to work hard in the temple and to serve the priests every way that I could.

"I soon learned that everyone in the temple was searching for the same peace, but none of them had received it. They were as unsatisfied as I was.

She continued: "I often wondered if there was anything else I could do to find peace in my heart. Many nights, I wept for hours in the darkness when no one could see me. I felt guilt and I knew no way to find the peace that I longed for. Not until I was 74 years old did I discover what I had sought all of my life."

Then she said: "The first time I listened to you, Mr. Osborn, when you talked about God loving me and sending His Son to die for me on the Cross, shedding His blood for the remission of my sins, I felt something happening inside of me. At last someone was showing me the way to find peace with God. I wept because I believed what you said about this Jesus. Without fully understanding your teaching, I believed it and I felt that my whole life was being washed clean.

"I repeated the prayer as you directed us. Wonderful peace came into my heart when I welcomed Jesus into my life. My mind and thoughts seemed to be cleansed. My heart was changed. I no longer felt guilt and shame before God. I felt I was sheltered in Jesus. I had never had such peace and joy. I knew I was *saved*. I was BORN AGAIN with the *Life* of Jesus.

"I threw away my Buddhist habits and acquired ordinary clothes to wear. I left the temple and returned to the village of my people. I wanted to share this Good News with them. I was changed forever.

"Now the rest of my life will be conse-crated to serving Jesus Christ, God's Son who is my Savior. I am so happy!"

That dear woman acquired a Bible and began to learn about the Christian faith. Not long after she returned to her people, she began to teach groups of them about the Lord and together, they built a bamboo and thatch meeting house which soon became a thriving church.

You will experience that peace with God while you are reading this book.

**B**uddhist Nun in Thailand who heard the Gospel during the open air Osborn Crusade, believed on Christ, was converted and began sharing her faith in her village. A new church resulted.

RELIGION can never re-generate a person. Rituals, ceremonies and creeds are superficial. But Jesus saves! His *Life* imparts A *new birth*!

Joining a church is not what saves a person. Only when one is *reborn* does he or she experience salvation from God.

# CHAPTER 3

# The Reborn Prostitute

THE NEW LIFE God offers is an abundant and miracle-*Life* — a miraculous *rebirth*. Jesus said: *I am come that you might have Life, and that you might have it more abundantly.* Joh.10:10

✧✧✧

DURING ONE OF our crusades in Latin America, a prostitute who was dying of cancer was hauled to our mass meeting in a wheelbarrow. Some Christians found her languishing on a straw mat on the ground of a small adobe hut where she had been abandoned to die.

When they told her about the crusade and offered to haul her there in the wheelbarrow, she was overwhelmed by their kindness. At first she objected because she was sure that there was no hope for her ruined

31

life. She had spent her years in prostitution and felt a terrible sense of guilt and shame.

The Christians convinced her that *God sent not His Son into the world to* **condemn** *the world; but that the world through Him might be* **saved**. Joh.3:17

They placed pillows in the old wheelbarrow and hauled her to the crusade. Her emaciated body resembled a sallow skin-covered skeleton, except for her swollen cancer-ridden abdomen.

Lying there on the wheelbarrow under the open sky, she listened to the message of new *Life* through Jesus Christ and how one can be *reborn* by receiving His *Life* into one's heart by faith. I remember well my subject that night.

I emphasized the *love* and compassion of Jesus Who died on the Cross to redeem us from our sins. I stressed the fact that His *Life* changes our nature and creates in us a new person; that it heals our diseases and regenerates us spiritually, mentally and physically. I reminded them that the Bible says to *forget not* **all** *of His benefits; Who forgives* **all** *of your iniquities; Who heals* **all** *of your diseases.*Psa.103:3

When we finished the message and led those thousands of people in a prayer of repentance and of acceptance of Christ, she could hardly believe that God loved her enough to forgive her and to impart His *Life* to her. She felt she had nothing to offer Christ but a deteriorated and hopelessly incurable body that had been used and abused in a life of sin.

The Christians encouraged her to *only believe*.Mar.5:36

At last, the realization of God's immeasurable *love* dawned upon her and she accepted His mercy and received Him into her heart.

Then came the glorious joy of pardon and forgiveness. New *Life* permeated her old nature. She was regenerated by the incomprehensible *Life* and Spirit of Jesus Christ. She was BORN AGAIN.

Lying in that wheelbarrow, weeping for joy and thanking God for His peace, she looked up at her friends, reached out her bony arms and they helped her to her feet — for the first time in weeks.

As they thanked God together, the dear woman was so overcome with joy and peace that she forgot about her cancer. She suddenly realized that the large tumor had disappeared and that her legs and arms had become strong.

The woman was not only purged of her sins and made clean by the blood of Jesus Christ, but she was miraculously healed. She had experienced *the new birth*.

She made her way through the press of people to the platform. I can still see her standing there weeping, with her bony arms raised toward heaven, and her up-turned face looking like that of an angel.

Her entire lifestyle was changed. *Old things had passed away; behold all things had become new.*[2Co.5:17]

She began attending one of the churches and became a faithful worker in the church. As she grew in her faith, she consecrated her life to winning other people to Jesus Christ.

What that woman received from God is the abundant *Life* that Jesus Christ came to share with each person who receives Him into his or her heart by faith

*The gift of God is Eternal Life.*[Rom.6:23]

This miraculous experience is called sal-vation, redemption, the *new birth*, being saved, becoming a new creature, a Christian, a believer, a follower of Christ.

It is the marvelous state of being reconciled to God. It is called a *new birth*, because Jesus said, *Except a person be* BORN AGAIN, *he or she cannot see the Kingdom of God. Marvel not that I said unto you, you must be* BORN AGAIN. Joh.3:3,7

◇◇◇

GOD IS NOW making it possible for you to know *How to be* BORN AGAIN by causing this book to be in your hands. You can be sure that before you have finished reading these chapters, you will receive His new *Life*.

As you learn about what Christ did for you in His death on the Cross, just believe that He did it for *you*. By embracing the facts of the Gospel, God's divine *Life* will be engendered in you through the living truth that you read.

Do not *try* to accept Christ or *try* to be BORN AGAIN. Just read, and believe. The good seed of divine truth will be planted in your life as you learn about it. Jesus Who *IS* the *Divine Truth* enters your life as you learn and believe what the Word of God

35

says about redemption. When the seed of Truth is planted in the soil of your believing heart, it engenders *"a new creature in Christ."* That will take place while you read.

Good seed grows and procreates by itself. You do not have to *try* to make it grow. All you have to do is to plant it in your heart.

Through knowledge of the Truth about what Christ did for you, you will be *saved,* as you believe that Truth. That is the same as to say, if you plant good seed in good soil, you will reap a good harvest.

You do not need to *try* to make the seed grow. It grows by its own life-power. In the same way, the seed of God's word grows by its own *Life*-power too. And its *Life*-power is *Supernatural.*

When speaking of the *new birth,* I like the word *saved* because the Bible says: *Christ Jesus came into the world to **save** sinners.*[1Ti. 1:15]

The word *saved* is a powerful biblical word that indicates a total miracle, a transformation that takes place in the life of any person who receives the Truth of Jesus Christ by faith.

It is a word that means to be forgiven, pardoned, saved, rescued, healed and made whole physically, mentally and spiritually; to be preserved, protected, watched over; to prosper and succeed; to have plenty and to live in abundance; to have eternal *Life;* to experience the miracle-*Life* of God.

Those are terms that express what takes place in the life of any person who believes on Jesus Christ, receives Him into their life by faith, and is miraculously BORN AGAIN.

◇◇◇

**A** BLIND HINDU villager was led to one of our crusades in India. He had been blind for over five years and had never heard the Gospel of Jesus Christ.

As we proclaimed the *Love* of God and how Christ suffered the penalty of our sins in our place, in order to redeem us, the blind man was intrigued and he listened attentively.

As we spoke about the Cross of Christ and recounted the story of His crucifixion, I emphasized the fact that *we* were the ones who should have been crucified, because *we* had sinned against God. But Christ's love for us caused Him to suffer the punishment that *we* deserved.

The blind man began to weep. He told us later, "I had never heard about this Christ before. It seemed very important to me. I felt like *The Omnipotent One* was amidst the multitude. I decided: I shall believe this teaching that they call Good News; I shall accept it! And when I made that decision, inside of me I felt like my sins were washed away. I could not understand it all, but when I thought of the blood of that good man, Jesus, I felt like I was being cleansed of my sins.

"I don't remember how long I remained squatted on the ground. I did not want to move. What I had heard caused me to have such peace that I wept. The young man who led me there did not know what to think. This Jesus seemed to be very near. I welcomed Him into my heart. I felt that all of my sins were forgiven.

"When I finally finished praying and crying, I opened my eyes and I could see everything clearly. Jesus had restored sight to my eyes that had been blind. What a powerful Savior He is! Thank you for telling me about Him! I am just a village farmer who was blind. Now I am a new man and I can see everything!"

No words can describe such a conversion. He was BORN AGAIN.

The power of the *Life* of Jesus Christ entering a human person is unlimited.

✧✧✧

**R**ELIGION CAN NEVER regenerate a person. Rituals, ceremonies and creeds are superficial and empty. But *Jesus saves!* His *Life* imparts a new birth! And that is what will happen to you while you read this book, if you *only believe.*

Real Christianity is not a religion; it is a *Life* – it is something that you can experience through the miracle of a *new birth.*

Joining a church is not what saves a person. One must be *reborn* to receive salvation from God.

This miracle will take place in you when you believe what the Bible says that Jesus did for you on the Cross. *Faith comes by hearing...the Word of God* Rom.10:17 – or by knowing what Christ accomplished on your behalf.

I have had the glorious privilege of helping tens of thousands of people to discover this miracle-*Life* and it can happen to you too.

39

So read with an open heart and be sensitive to the presence of God's Spirit because He is with you to convince you of *Truth* and to help you to believe for the salvation of your soul.

Jesus said, *I am the Way, the Truth and the Life.* Joh.14:6

Now I want to help you to better understand this *new birth*.

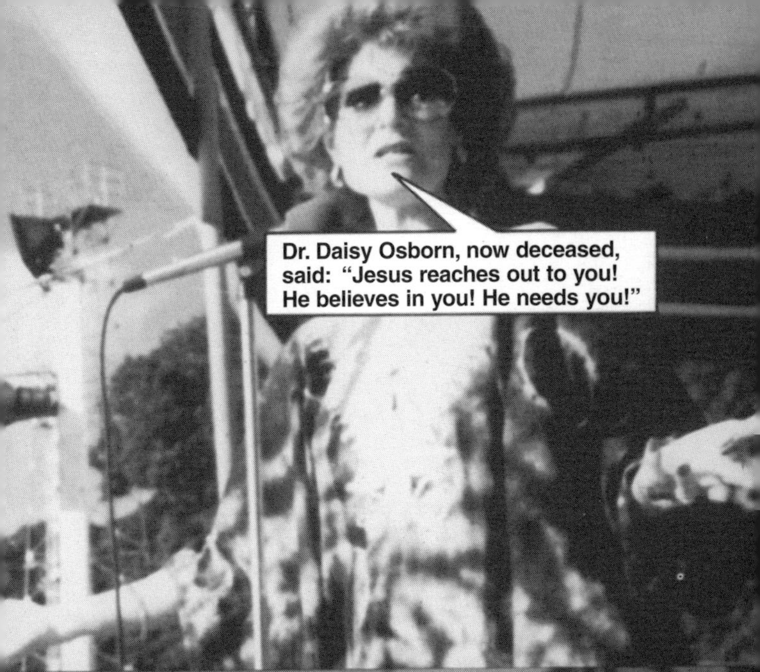
Dr. Daisy Osborn, now deceased, said: "Jesus reaches out to you! He believes in you! He needs you!"

T.L. Osborn says: "God loves you! He paid for you! He values you! He comes to you!"

YOU CAN be saved, or BORN AGAIN today! This book, in your hands, can guide you in receiving the greatest miracle possible, a *new birth*.

## CHAPTER 4

# Understanding The New Birth

**D**ID YOU EVER throw a rope to a drowning person and have him or her clutch it while you pulled them to safety? Did you ever save a life?

Did anyone ever save you from death?

Did you ever rescue someone from a burning building?

Are you saved? Have you been BORN AGAIN? (To be *saved* or to be BORN AGAIN means the same thing.) Do you know that if one dies without accepting Christ as Savior, that person is eternally separated from God?

The Bible says that *whoever was not found written in the Book of Life was cast into the lake of fire.*Rev.20:15

◇◇◇

**T**HE PURPOSE of this book is to help you to understand the *new birth*, how Christ's sacrificial death on the Cross makes this spiritual miracle possible and how you can be saved from your sins and diseases, from failure and poverty, from the evil of shame and guilt, from eternal death and separation from God.

Humankind was not made for a life of sin, disease, guilt and despair. When God created Adam and Eve, His plan was that they would share His divine *Life* and live in rapport with Him. But they sinned against Him by not respecting or believing what He said. Their sin resulted in their separation from Him and, consequently, all succeeding generations have been estranged from God.

*As by one, sin entered into the world, and death by sin; so death passed upon all, for that all have sinned.*[Rom.5:12]

But now, thank God, Christ has *come into the world to **save** sinners.*[1Ti.1:15] You can be saved today and reconciled to Him. You can believe on Jesus Christ, receive His new *Life* and experience a spiritual *rebirth*.

These next chapters will help you to understand what the miracle of the *new birth* can mean in your life.

YOU HAVE been born once—born in sin—a child of sin. Now Christ says: *Ye must be BORN AGAIN.* Joh.3:7 You must be converted—changed. To be saved, you must become *a new creature in Christ Jesus.* 2Co.5:17

## CHAPTER 5

# Become A
# Child of God

**W**HAT DOES it mean to be BORN AGAIN?

FIRST: The *new birth* means *TO BECOME A child of God.* The Bible says: *As many as received Christ, to them gave He power to become the sons* [and daughters] *of God.* Joh.1:12

Jesus said, *Ye must be BORN AGAIN.* Joh.3:7 This *new birth* is a miracle. Christ actually enters your life and you become a new person by the power of His presence in you. You have been born once — born in sin — a child of sin. Now Christ says: *Ye must be BORN AGAIN.* Joh.3:7 You must be converted — changed. To be saved, you must become *a new creature* in Christ Jesus.

*Being BORN AGAIN, not of corruptible seed, but of incorruptible, by the Word of God, which lives and abides for ever.*1Pe.1:23

The miracle of the *new birth* is experienced when one accepts Christ into his or her heart by faith. This miracle does not take place by accepting a religion; it is engendered in a person when they accept the Christ-*Life*—not a philosophy but a person, not a liturgy but a *Life*, not a religion but a reality, not by sharing a ceremony, but by becoming a *new creation*.

When I was married, I did not join the "marriage religion." I received a *person*—my wife, into my life. When I was BORN AGAIN, I did not join the "Christian religion." I received a *person*—the Lord Jesus Christ, into my life. My conversion was as definite as my marriage. On both occasions, another person became integral to my being.

The angel said: *Call His Name Jesus: for He shall **save** His people from their sins.*[Mat.1:21] When His divine *Life* is imparted to one who receives Christ by faith, the result is the *new birth*—SALVATION.

The Bible says: *God sent not His Son into the world to condemn the world; but that the world through Him might be **saved**.* [Joh.3:17] He desires that you comprehend His plan of redemption, that you receive His new *Life* and that you thereby experience a miraculous *rebirth* into the Family of God.

The biblical apostle, Peter, announced to the people that, *Whoever calls on the Name of the Lord shall be **saved*** [or BORN AGAIN].<sup>Acs. 2:21</sup>

Through the miracle of this *new birth,* one is delivered from the dominion of sin and is restored as a child of God, a member of His Divine Royal Family.

What else does it mean to experience the *new birth?*

HE WAS a bachelor who hated the idea of God. He resented all clergy persons. He despised the Church and avoided any contact with Christianity.

During the war, he served as a Dutch naval officer. In battles at sea, he had watched the bodies of sailors flung through the air by bomb explosions. He said he had shaken his fist toward heaven many times and cursed the idea of God, daring Him, if He existed, to strike him dead.

CHAPTER 6

# Revelation of Divine Love

**W**HAT DOES it mean to be BORN AGAIN?

SECOND: The *new birth* means the discovery that **God loves us like we are.** The biblical apostle Paul reminds us that *God commends his Love toward us, in that, while we were yet sinners, Christ died for us.*<sup>Rom.5:8</sup>

◇◇◇

**T**HE OWNER of a large hotel attended one of our mass crusades in Holland. Over 100,000 people gathered nightly on the Maleiveld—a huge open field at the center of The Hague. This man was curious about what was attracting so many Hollanders to these public Gospel meetings.

He was a bachelor for whom the idea of God was contemptible. He resented clergy persons and despised the Church, avoiding any contact with Christianity which he considered to be organized superstition.

During the war, he served as a Dutch naval officer. In battles at sea, he had watched the bodies of sailors flung through the air by bomb explosions. He said he had shaken his fist toward heaven many times, cursing the idea of God, daring Him, if He existed, to strike him dead.

He had boasted that he would never stoop in "religious superstition" to pray to a God that he did not believe existed.

Then came our crusade, affecting his nation. Curiosity finally provoked him to go assess for himself what so many of his fellow-citizens were talking about.

The night that he ventured into the crowd, I preached about the simplicity of prayer and of calling on the Name of the Lord to receive a new *Life* and to be BORN AGAIN.

He listened as I stressed the price that Jesus Christ had paid on the Cross for our salvation, giving His *Life* to ransom us from the dominion of sin. I explained that this miraculous *rebirth* made us God's children, and that being part of the Family of God, we could pray and receive the blessings that our Heavenly Father had provided for us.

✧✧✧

**I** EMPHASIZED the fact that if Christ had not laid down His *Life* to purge us from our sins, we would still be separated from God. But that He loves us so much that He gave His Son to die on the Cross on our behalf, to suffer the penalty of our transgressions, blotting out the record of our sins like a debt that is paid in full.

I remember how I was pressed in my spirit to tell the people that God paid the price to remove our sins that separated us from Him because He wanted us to be part of His Family. I kept stressing that **God loves us like we are.**

That man who resented Christianity so much, had never heard these Gospel facts. He hated the idea of God because he lacked information. To him, prayer was a superstitious ritual formulated by religious charlatans to attract people into their seductive webs. But as he listened, the dear man began to realize that a great price had been paid so that people can pray to God and receive His compassionate response to their needs.

IN CLOSING MY message that night in Holland, I stressed that *Whoever would call on the Name of the Lord would be saved;* <sup>Rom.</sup> <sup>10:13</sup> I emphasized that Jesus stands at the door of every human heart, knocking and waiting to enter and to share His *Life;* that the greatest miracle of prayer is when Jesus imparts His miracle-*Life* to someone and that person is *reborn* with new divine *Life* by receiving the Lord Jesus into his or her heart.

We prepared the multitude for prayer, and that man told us later: "I looked around and saw everyone bowing their heads to pray. So I asked myself: 'Can all of these fellow-Hollanders be crazy? Are they all deceived? Is it possible that there is something to this God that I have hated?'"

Then he added. "I told myself: 'If I ever expect to try praying a prayer to the God that I never believed existed, this ought to be my best opportunity. I'm going to do what this man says. If there is a God, then it seems to me that He would answer me here amidst so many people who claim to believe in Him!'"

So he placed his hands on his chest and looked up to pray and in that moment, he said that an overwhelming awareness of a *Divine Presence* gripped him. He reported:

"I had decided to pray. But the moment that I lifted my eyes, there before me stood Jesus Christ. I was so frightened that I wanted to hide myself. I thought He might have come to kill me because I had dared Him so often to strike me dead.

"But His eyes were fixed on mine and I seemed riveted there, unable to budge. He seemed to know every sin that I had committed and every blasphemy I had spoken. In a few seconds my whole lifetime passed before Him. Such fear and awe seized me that I dared not even blink.

"I felt the most reprehensible shame and remorse for the infamous and flagrant life I had lived and for the way I had cursed this man Jesus. Why had I so hated Him? What evil had He ever done to me? What made me doubt His existence?

"As He looked into the depths of my soul, I felt that my eyes would explode from the tears that poured from them. If He would only stop looking *into* me!

"After what seemed an interminable exposure of my stubborn hatred before His divine compassion, with His eyes riveted to mine, slowly but certainly a soft and tender smile appeared on the Savior's face. With that quiet gesture of *Love*, I knew He had not come to kill me, and that He did not hold my sins against me. What joy and what relief! I believed I was forgiven!

"As His smile became visible, He faded from my sight. My physical strength had dissipated and I sank to the ground, sobbing and weeping. I discovered that He loved me, despite my rebellion. He loved me *like I was*.

"The people around me were praising God. It seemed like heaven to me. The sound of the multitude was like a great waterfall as the voices of a hundred thousand Hollanders worshiped the God I had cursed all of my life.

"When I was able to get to my feet, I was a new creature. I was BORN AGAIN. The Lord Jesus was alive in me. I had received the divine gift of His new *Life*.

"I pressed my way through the multitude and mounted the platform to tell the public what had happened. But I could not speak because of weeping. The joy I felt was overwhelming. I was *reborn!*"

◇◇◇

AFTER WITNESSING this life-changing miracle, my wife and I discovered that we had been lodged in that man's hotel during our crusade. There was a large open garden right below our room that, when the weather was nice, served as a breakfast patio. The morning after that man's conversion, the people were eating outside. We had opened our windows to savor the fresh morning air.

A man's voice could be heard above the other noise. He was talking about Jesus. We looked out the window and saw that it was that dear man who had been converted. He was going from table to table, sharing his experience with Christ. He wanted every hotel guest to know that this Jesus is a living reality. The man was BORN AGAIN. He had become *a new creature.*[2Co.5:17]

He had made the great discovery that God loves us even before we love Him; He wants us even before we want Him; He comes to us even before we come to Him; He believes in us even before we believe in Him; He wants us near Him even before we want to have anything to do with Him.

◇◇◇

WHAT A MARVEL that anyone who believes on Christ and understands how and why He died to purge us from our sins, can receive this *new birth* and become a member of God's Royal Family.

When you comprehend Christ's sacrifice to save you, and when you receive Him into your life by faith, you become living proof that God loves each of us *like we are*. What a wonder of His grace and mercy!

In what other terms can the biblical *new birth* be understood?

*Biblical Salvation* is available to all who believe that Christ assumed the judgment of our sins to restore us to God as though we had never sinned. No crime can be punished twice. No debt can be paid twice. Christ acted on our behalf. He arose from the dead and returned to restore God's Life in us. *He took our sins in His own body on the cross.* 1Pe.2:24 *We have redemption through his blood.* Eph.1:7

"As you preached, you made me realize that I am the one who should have been crucified, because I was the one who had committed evil and had sinned against God and against people. Jesus was innocent. He had committed no sin.

"I found myself weeping. I wanted to cry out, 'Why YOU, Lord? Why are YOU the one Who was crucified? You committed no evil? I was the one they should have crucified! I am the guilty one!'"

# CHAPTER 7

# Killer Pardoned

**W**HAT DOES it mean to be BORN AGAIN?

THIRD: **I**T MEANS *that one's sins have been forgiven.* The Bible says: *He forgives all of our iniquities.*[Psa.103:3]

The angel said: *You shall call His Name Jesus: for He shall save His people from their sins.*[Mat.1:21]

God says: *I am He that blots out your transgressions…*[Isa.43:25] *Your sins and iniquities will I remember no more.*[Heb.10:17]

❖❖❖

**A** MAN ATTENDED one of our crusades in Latin America. From his youth, he hated protestant Christians, robbing them and destroying their crops or businesses or property. He and his friends would ambush Christian believers in the countryside, mug and rape them, plunder their belongings, and sometimes even murder them.

For some reason, that malevolent gangster attended our crusade. The night that he was present, I preached about what Christ's suffering on the cross means to us—how that in His crucifixion, He endured the judgment and penalty that *our sins deserved.*

For the first time in his life, that man realized that God had created us in His own image, to be His friends and partners in life. For the first time, he understood that, since God is *Love,* even though humanity sinned against Him, He found a way to redeem us—to save us—to give us a new beginning.

That man comprehended the fact that hatred, evil and murder are the effects of sin in human lives, that it is the destroyer—Satan who causes people to commit these evil deeds against others and against God, and that the penalty of sin is *death.*

Never before had that villain of a man realized that when Christ died on the cross, He assumed *our* penalty and suffered the judgment of *our* sins, and that if we believe on Him, we are declared *no longer guilty;*

that He gives us a new beginning. We are *saved*. We are BORN AGAIN.

That miserable man did not realize that sin was the abyss that separated humanity from God, nor that, despite human sins, God so desired fellowship with people that He offered His Son as a ransom to redeem us from our sins, and to open the *Way* for us to return to Him. The Cross of Christ suddenly became understandable to him— an event that had paid for his sins and had made his own salvation possible.

He told us later that, as he began to think about his hatred and shameful acts against innocent people, he realized that every evil deed he had committed helped nail Jesus to that Cross. He said that a reproachful and ghastly shame came over him as he saw the picture of Christ hanging there between two thieves, enduring the judgment that *his own sins* deserved.

When he reported his conversion, he said, "As you preached, you made me realize that *I* was the one who ought to have been crucified since it was *I* who had committed such evil acts. Jesus was innocent. He had not sinned.

"I was weeping and I wanted to cry out, 'Why *You*, Lord? Why did they crucify *You*? What evil did *You* ever commit? *I* am the one whom they should crucify! *I* am the one who is guilty!'"

✧✧✧

**W**HEN I INVITED the audience to accept Christ, that malicious persecutor of Christians rushed to the front of the arena, fell at the feet of Jesus, received Him by faith and was given a new beginning with a miracle infusion of God's divine *Life*. He was BORN AGAIN.

When the prayer was ended, the fact that overwhelmed him was that his sins were blotted out like a debt that was paid. In God's records, no account remained of his brutal and malicious deeds. The Bible says, *Their sins and their iniquities will I remember no more.*[Heb.8:12;10:17]

He had felt such guilt and remorse. Now his sins were purged and he knew that he was BORN AGAIN. He had experienced what Paul described as the *washing of regeneration, and renewing of the Holy Ghost.*[Tit.3:5]

✧✧✧

No WONDER John said that all glory be-
longs *unto HIM that loved us, and washed us
from our sins in His own blood.*<sup>Rev.1:5</sup> The
apostle Paul expressed that *In* [Christ] *we
have redemption through His blood; even the
forgiveness* [remission] *of sins.*<sup>Col.1:14</sup>

For those who believe on Christ and who
receive Him by faith, the condemning record of sin is wiped out. It is purged. No
account remains that can be held against
them.

*For Christ's death on the cross has made peace
with God for all by His blood...He has brought
you back as His friends...Now as a result Christ
has brought you into the very presence of God,
and you are standing there before Him with
nothing left against you...the only condition is
that you fully believe the Truth...convinced of
the Good News that Jesus died for you, and
never shifting from trusting Him to save you.*
Col.1:20-23LB

*There is therefore now no condemnation to
them which are in Christ Jesus,* <sup>Rom.8:1</sup> because
*who can lay anything to the charge of those who
have become God's children by faith in Christ?*
Rom.8:33

*As far as the east is from the west, so far has
He removed our transgressions from us.*<sup>Psa.103:12</sup>

Being BORN AGAIN means that *one's sins have been forgiven, blotted out and forever purged from our record.*

No religion on earth can offer that miraculous regeneration. It is wrought in us by the Holy Spirit when we comprehend God's *Love*, when we realize what Christ's death on the cross means for us, and when we receive Him by faith in our hearts.

The subject of our next chapter is a profound, life-changing example of what this *new birth* can mean in otherwise ruined lives.

"God never left Himself without a witness; there were always His reminders." Ac. 14:17 Living Bible
"He sent us to preach the Good News everywhere and to testify that ... everyone who believes in Him will have their sins forgiven through His name." Ac. 10:42,43 Living Bible

During more than a half-century, Dr. T.L. and his late wife, Dr. Daisy, ministered together carrying the Gospel to millions of people in over 80 nations of the world.

THE FATHER reached down and, in loving embrace, grasped his little son and daughter that he had treated with such vicious cruelty. Then, holding his children, he turned to embrace his wife whom he had often brutalized. The power of Christ had made him a new father. He was BORN AGAIN.

In tears, He said to his children: "You don't have to be afraid of Papa any more! Papa has found Jesus. He has a new life now. Papa won't hurt your Mommy any more. He loves Mommy and he loves you too!"

## CHAPTER 8

# Ricardo, I Am Jesus!

**W**HAT DOES it mean to be BORN AGAIN?

FOURTH: **It means that one *receives a new spiritual Life*.** The Bible says, *If anyone is in Christ, he* [or she] *is a new creature: old things are passed away; behold, all things become new.* 2Co.5:17

The apostle, John said: *We know that we have passed out of death into Life* 1Jo.3:14RV —a new kind of *Life* that is miraculously engendered by God in those who believe on Christ and who receive Him by faith.

What a wonder, to become *a new creature*—to receive a new spiritual *Life*—to be BORN AGAIN!

**I**N ONE OF our crusades abroad, a cruel and wicked young father was miraculously

69

converted. While we were proclaiming the Gospel to the multitude, the man actually heard the voice of the Lord calling to him.

He had become involved with some men of hostile and insidious character. Drinking and gambling consumed his money. His wife and two little children were left destitute. When he would come home, his children were horrified to see him beat their mother, throwing her to the floor and often kicking her like one might abuse an animal.

The father's cruelty became so injurious that the children would hide themselves under their house when they heard him coming home, while their mother cowered and cringed in fear.

She heard about our crusade and, with her children, took refuge in the multitude. The message of Good News brought hope and courage to her life.

Imagine her astonishment at what happened one night. After the message and after thousands had accepted Christ, we had prayed for those who were sick, and they had begun coming to the platform to report miracles that had been received.

This young mother, standing amidst the multitude, heard a man trying to tell what had happened to him. He was weeping so convulsively that he could hardly be understood. Suddenly, she realized that it was her husband. Something miraculous had happened.

She grabbed her children and rushed through the crowd to the platform. As she got near, she cried out, "Ricardo, Ricardo, it's me! I'm coming! The children are with me! Ricardo, it's me!"

The man heard her voice just as she mounted the steps, half dragging her little frightened children. She rushed toward him and they fell into each other's arms weeping together.

The father reached down and in loving embrace, grasped his children in his arms. Then, turning to his wife, he told his little son and daughter: "You don't have to be afraid of Papa any more. Papa has found Jesus. He has a new life now. Papa won't hurt Mommy any more. He loves Mommy and he loves you too!"

✧✧✧

WHAT A MIRACLE! Wiping his tears and still sobbing, that ex-abusive father told the audience about his sinful life and what had happened to him.

He had come to the crusade as a pickpocket. He was standing in a dark area sheltered by a large tree. As we preached about Christ and His presence, from the top of the tree he had heard a voice like a trumpet saying: *"Ricardo, I am Jesus. Follow Me!"*

He had been so stunned and frightened by the voice that he wanted to escape from the crusade because he thought his sense of guilt was making him imagine things. Then, just as he started to leave, the voice repeated the same words: *"Ricardo, I am Jesus. Follow Me!"*

Realizing that the Lord was calling him to repentance, he had fallen to the ground, weeping in shame for his sins. There, he had realized Christ's mercy and pardon and had accepted Him as Savior. Then he had come to the platform to tell the multitude about his experience.

He was a new man—regenerated—BORN AGAIN through the *Life* of Jesus Christ. He became a faithful member of one of the churches where he and his wife have been serving the Lord in Christian ministry.

◇◇◇

THAT IS THE new spiritual *Life* I am trying to make clear in this book.

That is what happens when He *saves* a person—when one is BORN AGAIN. A conversion takes place. Old desires, habits, diseases and failures pass away. The Bible says, *"All things become new."* One receives a new *Life*, a new nature, new health, new desires, new ambitions. Christ's *Life* becomes integral to that person.

The Bible says, *A new heart also will I give you, and a new spirit will I put within you: I will take away the stony heart out of your flesh, and I will give you a heart of flesh. I will put my spirit within you, and cause you to walk in My statutes.* Eze.36:26-27

Jesus said: *I am come that you might have Life...more abundantly.* Joh.10:10

Being BORN AGAIN means that we have received this new spiritual *Life* from God. His miracle-*Life* is being imparted to you while you are reading this book.

Now I want to explain further what it means when one receives the *new birth*.

📖

He had never married, and had abused little girls to satisfy his lustful passions. He cheated and lied in business and lived a wasteful and contemptible life.

His guilt before God caused him to tremble with fear as he realized that the penalty of sin is death. Then he began to comprehend the reason for Christ's death on the Cross.

# CHAPTER 9

# The Moslem Trader

**W**HAT DOES it mean to be BORN AGAIN?

FIFTH: **I**T **MEANS TO** *RECEIVE PEACE* **wiTh God.**
Jesus said: *Peace I leave with you. My peace I give unto you.* Joh.14:27 He added, *I have spoken unto you, that in Me ye might have peace.* Joh. 16:33

Real peace only comes when one is aware that all punishment for one's sin has been suffered by Christ in His death on the Cross.

The Bible says, *God showed His great love for us by sending Christ to die for us while we were still sinners...now...He has declared us* **not guilty***...Now we rejoice in our wonderful new relationship with God — all because of what our Lord Jesus Christ has done in dying for our sins — making us* **friends of God.** Rom.5:8-9,11LB

That is what the *new birth* means—experiencing real *peace with God.*

One who lives in sin can never experience the peace that comes by knowing that our sins have already been punished, and that, therefore, there is nothing on record to condemn the one who trusts in Christ.

The Bible says: *There is **no peace**, says my God, to the wicked.* Isa.57:21 But the Biblical apostle Paul said, *being justified by faith, we have **peace** with God through our Lord Jesus Christ.* Rom.5:1 *We were brought back to God by the death of His Son...*[and now] *we are His friends, and He is living within us!* Rom.5:10LB That is what it means to be BORN AGAIN—to have *peace with God.*

✧✧✧

**A** MOSLEM TRADER from Syria settled in Ghana for business reasons. He attended our crusade in the capitol city of Accra. Coming from a Moslem community, the Gospel that he heard in our crusade was his first experience of realizing what the Christian faith is all about.

He had never married, and had abused little African girls to satisfy his lustful passions. He was dishonest in business and lived a debauched and profligate life of immorality.

Finally, a dehumanizing stroke of paralysis left one side of his body limp and useless. In that debilitated condition he attended our crusade, dragging his paralyzed leg with the aid of a crutch while one arm dangled like a wet rope at his side.

We preached about how God loved the world so much that He gave His only Son to redeem us from sin and to destroy the consequences of sin in our lives. This was almost too marvelous for that man to comprehend.

Moslems are never told about God's *Love*. To them, *Allah* is a God of power and of wrath. They are never taught about His *Divine Love*.

That paralyzed Moslem listened. The destructiveness of his sins began to dawn upon him, as he began to realize the price Christ had paid to redeem humankind.

The knowledge that Jesus was crucified to suffer the punishment which *we ought to have suffered*, finally produced in that man sorrow and deep repentance for his life of sin. He began to feel shame and remorse for his corrupt and depraved life. He began to weep for his sins and to cry out to God for mercy. His guilt caused him to tremble with fear as he realized that the final penalty of sin is death.

The man began to comprehend the reason for the Cross of Christ. Jesus had assumed the penalty and had endured the judgment of the man's own despicable sins, so that he could have *peace* with God and be free of condemnation and guilt before Him.

He realized, at last, that God had created humankind in His own image and that no person could ever find peace while sinning against God. The glorious change came to him when he realized that Christ had died and that His blood had been shed to wash away the terrible sins that he had committed, to save him from the penalty of death.

As he cried out to God, an indescribable *peace* came to him and he said, "My fear and guilt were gone. I felt confidence in God's presence. I was no longer afraid of His wrath. I realized that at the Cross, Jesus suffered my punishment in my place and therefore the record of my sins was purged. I was free and forgiven. I was no longer afraid or guilty. I had *peace* with God. My sins were gone. I was BORN AGAIN."

He had stood amidst that multitude of people, weeping with gratitude for Salvation. Overwhelmed by the discovery that the Lord loves even the worst of sinners, he had not thought about his paralysis. He was so elated and exuberant about being *reborn* and about receiving a new beginning with God who loved him, that he had forgotten about his physical condition.

When at last the man regained his composure, he realized that his loathsome paralysis had disappeared. He rubbed the side of his face that had been sagged and twisted. It felt perfect. His hand, arm and leg were restored to normalcy. The man had been healed by Christ at the same time that he had received *peace* with God through the *new birth*.

He came to the platform to tell everyone what had happened, and to publicly express his new faith in Jesus Christ.

He wept as he showed the audience how his paralysis was gone. But he seemed even more astounded that his guilt and condemnation were gone. He had discovered *peace* with God. As a Moslem, he had only known the wrath of Allah. Now he knew about the *Love* of God. He would never again live in fear of God's wrathful judgment, but he would live in *peace*.

◇◇◇

THE BIBLE SAYS, *You were lost, without God, without hope. But now you belong to Christ Jesus, and though you once were far away from God, now you have been brought very near to Him because of what Jesus Christ has done for you with His blood. For Christ Himself is our way of* **peace**...*Now you are no longer strangers to God and foreigners to heaven, but you are members of His very own family, citizens of His country, and you belong in His household.* Eph.2:12-14,19LB

The moment you believe on Jesus Christ, you are justified before God and you have *peace* with Him. No one can lay anything to your charge Rom.8:33 when God has justified you Rom.3:24-26 and purged the record of your sins through the blood of His Son. Col.1:20

That is why you can have real *peace* with God, and it is why you can receive that *peace* right now. The Bible says, *Believe on the Lord Jesus Christ, and you shall be saved.* Acs.16:31

Being BORN AGAIN means to receive *peace* with God. No religion or ritual or ceremony or act of penance on earth can procreate that *peace* with God in one's life.

I could share many stories depicting what this *new birth* means in human lives. This next chapter will illustrate in another way the wonder of this experience.

📖

For FOURTEEN YEARS he had slept on the streets and lived out of garbage containers and in gutters. His clothes were filthy and ragged; his beard and hair were long and matted like an animal's.

No wonder the Bible says, *Who is like unto the Lord our God...He raises up the poor out of the dust, and lifts the needy out of the dunghill; that He may set him* [or her] *with princes.* Psa.113:7

# CHAPTER 10

# The Insane Beggar

**W**HAT DOES it mean to be BORN AGAIN?

SIXTH: **It means to be *restored to fellowship with God.*** You were created in God's likeness so that you can walk and talk with Him. *But your iniquities have separated between you and your God and your sins have hid His face from you that He will not hear.*<sup></sup>Isa. 59:2

Now instead of *fellowship* with the Father, people fear God. The thought of facing Him frightens them. They are condemned by their sins that mark them as guilty before Him.

But Jesus Christ *His own self took our sins in His own body on the tree, that we, being dead to sins, should live unto righteousness.*[1Pe. 2:24]

*There is therefore now no condemnation to them who are in Christ Jesus.* [Rom.8:1]

Only Christ can save us from our sins. We can only be BORN AGAIN by the miracle-*Life* of Christ being received by faith into our heart. He laid down His *life* and died on the Cross in order to purge our life of every sin and to bring us back to God as if we had never sinned. Jesus Christ *was slain, and has redeemed us to God by His blood.*<sup>Rev.5:9</sup>

That is why we can be restored to *fellowship* with God. That means that when we have received Jesus into our life by faith, and when we believe that He gave His *life* as a ransom to bring us back to God, then we can say with John: *Truly our fellowship is with the Father, and with His Son Jesus Christ.* <sup>1Jo.1:3</sup>

Thenceforth, He will be *a friend that sticks closer than a brother.* <sup>Pro.18:24</sup>

◇◇◇

A N INSANE BEGGAR possessed of evil spirits for fourteen years, attended one of our Latin American crusades. No one knows why or how the poor man found his way to our meeting.

He had slept in the streets and lived out of garbage containers. His clothes were filthy and ragged; his beard and hair were long and matted.

As that poor man stood at the far edge of the multitude, when the prayer was prayed for the salvation of sinners, the Lord Jesus suddenly appeared to him. He pointed His finger at the demon-possessed man and commanded the evil spirits to leave him and to enter him no more. At that moment, the man became perfectly sane and normal, and he resolved to follow Christ.

God had delivered him from evil spirits so he could be made part of His Royal Family. What a wonder that God would desire friendship and *fellowship* with someone who had been a human outcast for fourteen years.

The man was anxious to tell the multitude what had happened to him so he pressed through the crowd to the steps of the platform. But the ushers refused to let him mount the steps because they knew him as the insane beggar in their town. So the man went to the other side of the platform but the ushers had signaled their colleagues and he was refused again.

Fortunately, after the meeting that night, some Christians saw him and realized that he had been visited by the Lord. They took him to their house where he could bathe. The next day, they bought him new clothes, a barber shaved him and cut his hair, then they brought him back to the great crusade that evening. He looked like a Christian gentleman.

Not knowing who the man was, the ushers allowed him to come on to the platform that night, along with others, to witness of what Christ had done.

The dear man tried to speak but broke into tears. Finally he regained his composure enough to say to the people: "If you knew who I am, your ushers would not have allowed me to tell you what Christ has done in my life.

"I am the beggar who has slept on the ground and has eaten from the garbage containers of your town for fourteen years. I lived that way because I was possessed by evil spirits that tried to destroy me. I did not want to live as I did but demons controlled me. I cannot explain it, but they were in charge of everything that I did.

"I don't know why I came here last night. But when the prayer was prayed, I saw Jesus and He commanded the evil spirits to leave me. The instant He spoke, I was free. Oh, friends, I am free.

"Look at me! I am no longer the beggar who has eaten from your garbage containers and slept on your streets. Tonight, I have been given a new life by the power of Jesus Christ. I am now a child of God. I am your brother. Jesus loves me. I am saved!"

That dear man was regenerated. He was BORN AGAIN. He could have *fellowship* with God as intimately as any believer could have. He was healed and delivered, spiritually, mentally and physically.

That is what the Bible calls *salvation.* You can be sure that God is coming to you, while you are reading this book, helping you to embrace these truths and to experience His new *Life* being created in you by the power of the seed-Truth that is being planted in you as you read.

◇◇◇

WE HAVE BEEN privileged to witness the healing and restoration of many insane persons like that man, in many nations of the world. Christ healed them in Bible days and He has not changed.

During our recent crusade in Abidjan, Ivory Coast, over 130,000 people attended each meeting. One night, three insane men from three different towns, were brought to our meeting with both feet and hands bound. They were miraculously healed the same night, completely restored to their right minds.

No wonder the Bible says, *Who is like unto the Lord our God...He raises the poor out of the dust, and lifts the needy from the dunghill; that He may set them with the princes of His people.* Psa.113:5-8

Human persons were not made for a life of isolation and abandonment, of sin and disease. They were made to walk with God, in health, peace and dignity. But sin became the impenetrable barrier between Him and humanity. Isa.59:2

To open the *Way* for us to be restored to God, Christ's blood was *shed...for the remission of sins.* Mat.26:28 *If we confess our sins* [to Him], *He is faithful and just to forgive us our sins, and to cleanse us from all unrighteousness.* 1Jo.1:9

Now that Jesus laid down His *Life* as a ransom to redeem us from sin, we can now be restored to *fellowship* with God. We can now stand before Him without any sense of fear, guilt, shame or inferiority because of what Christ did through His death on the Cross for us.

The Bible says that Jesus Christ, *by Himself, **purged our sins**, [and] sat down on the right hand of the Majesty on high.* Heb.1:3

With our sins purged from the record, we can again walk and talk with God in the garden of His presence, like Adam and Eve did before they committed the original sin and were banished from His presence.

*Salvation is not a reward for the good we have done* Eph.2:9LB *...It is God Himself who has made us what we are and has given us new lives from Christ Jesus* v.10 *...You were lost, without God, without hope. But now you belong to Christ Jesus, and though you once were far away from God, now you have been brought very near to Him because of what Jesus Christ has done for you with His blood.* vs.12-13

BORN AGAIN—being *saved* means that one has regained true *fellowship* with God!

✧✧✧

# HOW TO BE BORN AGAIN

IN THESE NEXT chapters, I will elucidate the basic facts that make the *new birth* possible in one's life. These pages will help you to understand the simplicity of salvation. As you embrace these powerful facts, the miracle of the *new birth* will take place in your life.

*"Listen to me, and you will have a LONG, GOOD LIFE. Carry out my instructions, for they will lead you to REAL LIVING."* Prov. 4:10,13 Living Bible

*"How Excellent is your lovingkindness, O God! ... (to those who) put their trust under your wings. They shall be abundantly satisfied, they shall drink of the river of YOUR pleasure. For with YOU is the fountain of LIFE."* Psalm 36:7-9

Discover HIS *Good Life*. Live in harmony with God. Get His ideas. Work with His projects. See LIFE as He sees it. Discover who YOU are and YOUR own value. See yourself as God sees you. Live interested in His plans. He believes in YOU and treasures YOUR companionship.

To SAY, "I think I am saved; I try to be saved, but I'm not sure about it," is like saying, "I think I am married; I try to be married, but I'm not sure about it."

According to the Bible, when you know the simple truths that make salvation possible and you embrace them in word and in deed, you can be certain that you have been BORN AGAIN.

# CHAPTER 11

# Of This, You Can Be Sure

THE BIBLE SAYS, *We **know** that we have passed from death unto Life.* [1Jo.3:14] There are many things that we may never know. But we can *know* that we have received Christ's miracle-*Life*—that we are *saved*—that we are BORN AGAIN.

Many people ask, "How can I know that I am saved—that my sins are forgiven?"

The keeper of the jail at Philippi asked, *Sirs, what must I do to be **saved**?* [Acs.16:30] Paul and Silas responded, *Believe on the Lord Jesus Christ, and you shall be saved.* [Acs.16:31]

To say, "I do not know for sure if I am saved," is like saying, "I do not know for sure if I am married."

To say, "I think I am saved; I try to be saved, but I am not sure about it," is like saying, "I think I am married; I try to be married, but I am not sure about it."

When the basic truths of redemption are known, and when steps are taken to embrace those truths, one's *new birth* can be as certain as one's marriage.

The biblical apostle Paul said, *If you confess with your mouth the Lord Jesus, and believe in your heart that God has raised Him from the dead, you shall be **saved**.* Rom.10:9

When we do what the Holy Scriptures tells us, then we receive what those Scriptures promise. We can know that we have received Christ, that we have been *saved*, that we have been BORN AGAIN. This is not accepting the Christian *religion;* this is receiving the Christ-*Life*.

I have posed some questions for you to ponder, in an attempt to help you to assess your own faith for receiving Christ's miracle-*Life*.

**T.L.** and daughter LaDonna are bringing hope and faith to tens of thousands across the ex-Soviet Union who have known nothing but Godless communism.

**O**sborns bring the Gospel of Christ to thousands of Ukrainains.

IF YOU CAN answer "Yes" to these questions, then you will *know*, on the authority of God's Word, that you have received Christ and that you have become a child of God, that you have eternal *Life*, that you are BORN AGAIN.

# CHAPTER 12

# The Mystery Revealed

ACCORDING TO the Bible, a person who is BORN AGAIN 1) has come to God as a lost sinner, 2) has accepted by faith the Lord Jesus Christ as his or her personal Savior, by surrendering to Him as Lord and Master, 3) has confessed Christ as his or her Lord before the world, and 4) strives to please Him in every thought and word and deed.

Have you come to God realizing that you have been a sinner? Have you accepted the Lord Jesus Christ as your personal Savior? Are you aware that the judgment of sin is death? Do you believe that Christ has assumed the guilt and suffered the judgment of your sins, Isa.53:5-6 that He bore them, in *your* place, as *your* substitute, 1Pe.2:24 and that those sins are now remitted—that they are purged because He paid *your* penalty and died in *your* stead?

Have you welcomed Him into your life as your Lord and Master, ready to do His will even when it conflicts with your own?

Have you confessed that you believe that Christ bore the penalty of *your* sins, and that therefore you accept Him as your Savior and Master before the world?

Have you resolved to try to please Him in everything that you think and do and say?

If you can answer *"Yes"* to these questions that I have posed, then you can *know*, on the authority of God's Word, that you have become a *child of God*, [Joh.1:12] that you now have eternal *Life*. [Joh.3:36] You can be sure that God has imparted to you His *Life* and divine nature [2Pe.1:4] and that He has come to live in you. [Joh.14:23]

◇◇◇

THIS EXPERIENCE of being BORN AGAIN is what the Bible calls the greatest *mystery* known in Christianity. The apostle Paul said, *it is the* **mystery** *that has been hid from ages and from generations, but now is made manifest to His people.*[Col.1:26] He explains that this age-long *mystery* can be expressed in three words: *Christ in you.* Col.1:27

Jesus said, *Those who love me, will keep my words; and my Father will love them, and we will come to them, and make our **abode** with them.* Joh.14:23

Paul said, *Christ **lives** in me.* Gal.2:20 In another biblical verse, he said that when we believe on Christ and receive Him into our hearts by faith, we become *a **habitation** of God through His Spirit.* Eph.2:22 He expressed it another way saying that *if **Christ be in you**...the Spirit of Him that raised up Jesus from the dead **dwells in you**.* Rom.8:11

◇◇◇

IF YOU ARE NOT yet sure that you have accepted Christ into your heart and that you have surrendered your life to Him, or that you have confessed Him as your Lord and Master, then the next chapters will guide you to *peace* with God and to the miraculous experience of being BORN AGAIN.

I am sharing here some simple but fundamental truths for anyone who has a desire to respond to God's mercy and to be delivered from sin, from disease and pain, from poverty and need, from defeat and failure and from eternal death.

I suggest the following:

(a)  Fix a special time, in a quiet place, where you can ponder these truths alone with God.

(b)  Ask for the help of the Holy Spirit that is promised to those who seek Him.

(c)  Consider each truth and be sure that it is clearly understood and accepted.

(d)  Before you have finished reading these truths, you will know that your sins are forgiven, that you have received the Christ-*Life*, and have experienced being BORN AGAIN.

**OSBORN CRUSADES**

Ponce, Puerto Rico

Lubumbashi, R.D. Congo

Cabanatuan, Philippines

Kampala, Uganda

Madurai, India

Lagos, Nigeria

Jakarta, Indonesia

San Fernando, Trinidad

WHEN ONE decides that his or her own righteousness is sufficient and that they are capable of standing before God on the merits of their own goodness, that person is repudiating His mercy and grace, disregarding His *Love* and discrediting the vicarious sufferings of Christ on the Cross.

# CHAPTER 13

# The Abyss That Separates

THE PRINCIPAL TRUTH that must be embraced, before one can be BORN AGAIN is that *All have sinned and come short of the glory of God;*[Rom.3:23] that *your sins have separated between you and your God, and your iniquities have hid His face from you.*[Isa.59:2]

Sin is the abyss that separates one from God and from His divine blessings.

Before anyone can experience the *new birth*, that person must realize that he or she was first born in sin.

*As by one man* [Adam], *sin entered into the world, and death by sin; so death passed upon all people, for that all have sinned.*[Rom.5:12]

The Bible says, *All unrighteousness is sin.* It defines the sins that violate God's *Lifestyle* and that result in eternal separation from Him.

Jesus said: *From out of the heart, proceed evil thoughts, adulteries, fornications, murders, thefts, covetousness, wickedness, deceit, lasciviousness, an evil eye, blasphemy, pride, foolishness: all these evil things come from within, and defile the person.* Mar.7:21-23

Here is another list:

*Being filled with all unrighteousness, fornication, wickedness, covetousness, maliciousness; full of envy, murder, debate, deceit, malignity, whisperers, backbiters, haters of God, despiteful, proud, boasters, inventors of evil things, disobedient to parents, without understanding, covenant breakers, without natural affection, implacable, unmerciful: who knowing the judgment of God, that they which commit such things are worthy of death, not only do the same, but have pleasure in them that do them.* Rom.1:29-32

The Bible gives us yet another list:

*Know ye not that the unrighteous shall not inherit the Kingdom of God? Be not deceived: neither fornicators, nor idolaters, nor adulterers, nor effeminate, nor abusers of themselves with mankind, nor thieves, nor covetous, nor drunkards, nor revilers, nor extortioners, shall inherit the Kingdom of God.* 1Co.6:9-10

Then there is a biblical definition of sin:

104

*Now the works of the flesh are manifest, which are these: adultery, fornication, uncleanness, lasciviousness, idolatry, witchcraft, hatred, variance, emulations, wrath, strife, seditions, heresies, envyings, murders, drunkenness, revellings and...they which do such things shall not inherit the Kingdom of God.* Gal.5:19-21

God gave us the Ten Commandments, then He established His law that *the soul that sins shall surely die.* Eze.18:4 Therefore *the Scripture has concluded all under sin* Gal.3:22 and *if we say we have no sin, we deceive ourselves, and the truth is not in us.*1Jo.1:8

The biblical prophet Isaiah said, *All we like sheep have gone astray; we have turned everyone to his* [or her] *own way* Isa.53:6 and *we are all as an unclean thing, and all our righteousnesses are as filthy rags.* Isa.64:6

✧✧✧

So IT IS vital that a person be honest before God. As David said: *If You, Lord, should mark iniquities, who could stand?* Psa.130:3

Paul, the New Testament apostle, explains that one who is not BORN AGAIN *is darkened in understanding, alienated from the Life of God because of ignorance and the hardening of one's heart.* Eph.4:18RV

The first book of the Bible records the state of that early generation: *God saw that their wickedness was great on earth, and that every imagination of their thoughts was only evil continually...for all flesh had corrupted their way upon the earth.* Gen.6:5,12 A great Bible prophet said, *The heart is deceitful above all things, and is desperately wicked: who can know it?* Jer.17:9

The apostle Paul was a very religious man before receiving Christ as Savior, but despite his religious fervor, he came to realize that he had lived his life, alienated from God because of his sin, and that all of his religious piety could do nothing to absolve him of his sins.

*For we ourselves also were foolish, disobedient, deceived, serving diverse lusts and pleasures; living in malice and envy, hateful, and hating one another.* Tit.3:3 *We also once lived in the lusts of our flesh, doing the desires of the flesh and of the mind; and were by nature the children of wrath.* Eph.2:3RV

◇◇◇

So TO BE BORN AGAIN, the principal truth that one must face is that *sin is the impenetrable separation between people and God.* Men and women, without Jesus Christ, are lost and are living under the impending sentence of eternal death.

*For the wages of sin is death.*<sup></sup>Rom.6:23 *The soul that sins, it shall die.* Eze.18:4 *No one can by any means redeem his brother* [or sister], *nor give to God a ransom for them.*Psa.49:7 *Neither their silver nor their gold shall be able to deliver them…*Zep.1:18

Therefore, to be reconciled and reunited with God — to be BORN AGAIN into His Royal Family, one must realize that sin separates him or her from God and from all of the good that He wills for those whom He has created.

The worst possible sin is to reject God's immeasurable *Love*, to ignore the sacrifice of Christ, to refuse the ransom He has paid for our lives and to disbelieve or to disregard the greatest story ever told — the redemption of humanity through His death on the Cross.

◇◇◇

**W**HEN ANYONE decides that his or her own righteousness is *enough*, that they are capable of standing before God on the merits of their own goodness, they are repudiating the mercy and grace of God.

The biblical prophet Isaiah said: *We are all as an unclean thing, and all our righteousnesses are as filthy rags.* Isa.64:6

Jesus said, *The Pharisee stood and prayed thus, God, I thank You, that I am not as other people, extortioners, unjust, adulterers, or even as this publican. I fast twice in the week, I give tithes of all that I possess.* Luk.18:11-12 He trusted in the merits of his own religion. There was no shame or remorse in him.

But *the publican...would not lift up so much as his eyes to heaven, but smote upon his breast, saying, God be merciful to me a sinner.* Luk.18:13

Jesus said: *This publican was **justified** rather than the Pharisee: because those who exalt themselves shall be abased; and they who humble themselves shall be exalted.* Luk.18:14

So, in order to receive the *Life* of Jesus Christ, there are no human merits to justify a person before God. Sin is the great separator between humanity and deity.

But for the person who wants to be reconciled to God and to live in peace with Him, the *Way* is open and I want to share that truth with you next.

**OSBORN CRUSADE–Central Africa**

Since the demise of Dr. T.L. Osborn's wife, his daughter, Dr. LaDonna, now Vice-President and CEO of the Osborn World Ministry, is involved in seminars, mass crusades and Church-growth around the world. When possible, she shares with her father in Gospel campaigns like this one in Central Africa. Because *"the Gospel is the power of God unto salvation to everyone that believes,"* their life-mission is sharing Christ and His love globally, which they consider to be the ministry nearest the heart of God.

REPENTANCE means understanding that the suffering of Jesus Christ on the Cross was because of *our* sins. When we understand that His death was on our behalf, that realization produces *repentance* which is sorrow for our sins, with a resolve to change our attitude and our lifestyle accordingly.

# CHAPTER 14

# New Perspective

THIS NEXT TRUTH essential to being BORN AGAIN is to understand the cost and the consequences of sin, and thereby to change one's thinking—one's attitude about it. *The Bible calls that process* **repentance**.

When we know that God came to our human level in order to lift us from our fallen state; when we know that He gave His only Son to ransom us from the dominion of sin; when we know that He loved us so much that He could not leave us to suffer the guilt and condemnation, the disease and sickness, the poverty and failure, the loneliness and deterioration that are the consequences of our sins; when we know that Jesus took upon Himself all of our evil and died in our place—when we know those truths, *if we believe them and embrace them,* we experience a deep and profound sorrow for our sins. That is called *repentance!*

The Good News of the Bible is that God so loved us that He gave His Son to assume *our* guilt, to suffer *our* penalty, to endure the judgment of *our* sins and to die in *our* stead. He did this in order to give us Eternal *Life* and to restore us to Him as His friends and partners.

*Repentance* means understanding that the suffering of Jesus Christ on the Cross was because of *our* sins. When we understand that His death was on *our* behalf, that realization produces *repentance* — sorrow for our sins, and it produces a resolve to change our attitude and our lifestyle accordingly.

The Bible says, *For godly sorrow works **repentance** to salvation.*²Co.7:10

*Now God commands all people everywhere to* **repent**.Acs.17:30

Peter's message was: ***Repent**, and be baptized everyone of you in the name of Jesus Christ for the remission of your sins...*Acs.2:38

The Bible says that the followers of Jesus *went out and preached that people should **repent**.* Mar.6:12 It says of Jesus' ministry, *From that time He began to preach, and to say, **re-***

*pent*: *for the Kingdom of heaven is at hand.* <sup>Mat. 4:17</sup>

Christ paid the price to redeem us from our sins. He died on the Cross to ransom us from the jurisdiction of the slave master, Satan.

*Greater love has no one than this, that one would lay down his* [or her] *life for their friends.* <sup>Joh.15:13</sup> Jesus Christ did that for you and for me.

*God commends His love toward us, in that, while we were yet sinners, Christ died for us.* Rom.5:8

It was *our* sins that He bore on the Cross, *our* punishment that He suffered, *our* guilt and shame that He endured. You and I ought to have been crucified, but *Christ died for the ungodly.* Rom.5:6 He died for you and for me.

⬦⬦⬦

*R*EPENTANCE MEANS to change one's mind — one's perspective, to turn around. It indicates both Godly sorrow about one's sins, and a resolute change of purpose and of action in life.

When it becomes clear that pain and heartache, sorrow and failure, disease and plague, depression and poverty—and spiritual death itself (separation from God) are *due to sin*, then one's mind and attitude are changed profoundly.

Instead of assuming that we are doing no harm in our private life of sin, we discover that we are not only damaging our own life but our home, our family, our friends and our community. We realize that sin is the cause of sorrow, it scars lives, breaks homes, kills children, slays the body and damns the soul.

Jesus died on the Cross for you and for me, to pay for our sin. Pondering that pre-eminent truth engenders deep *repentance* in one's spirit.

Jesus said: *Except ye **repent**, ye shall all likewise perish.*[Luk.13:3,5]

Our salvation is based entirely on the grace (the unmerited favor) of God. No one can earn His favor by good works. Forgiveness and justification are available only because Jesus Christ assumed *our* guilt and bore the judgment that *our* sins merited.

✧✧✧

**B**IBLICAL *REPENTANCE* does not mean to simply regret sins or **to feel apologetic**

about them. It is a strong word that means to change or to turn about face. It signifies a complete revolution in one's attitude.

Repentance means that one turns around and starts walking in the opposite direction, as the Prodigal Son who wasted his life in *riotous living,* but who *came to himself,* and made a decision to get out of the hog pen and return to his father's house. In deep humility and sorrow he turned around and went home and said, *Father I have sinned against you.* [Luk.15:15-21] That is *repentance!*

There are numerous biblical accounts of people who *repented.* Job realized his sins, and said: *I abhor myself.* [Job.42:6] Isaiah said, *Woe is me! I am a man of unclean lips.*[Isa.6:5] Peter cried: *I am a sinful man.*[Luk.5:8] Paul called himself *the chief of sinners.*[1Ti.1:15]

Every sin that one has ever committed has become part of one's record and only Christ's blood can purge that record. He is doing that for you right now while you ponder the truths of these pages. Why? Because you are discovering that sin is what has separated you from God, and you realize the price that Christ has paid to redeem you. Knowing those truths produces a sense of profound biblical *repentance*.

◇◇◇

GOD IS AT WORK in your life right now. The chapters that follow will bring great peace and satisfaction to you as biblical faith fills your heart and you become confident that you are BORN AGAIN.

📖

LaDonna & T.L. strategize global crusades and literature-distribution. Their preaching is always confirmed by miracles. TONS of their books seed church leaders and believers for spiritual harvests, impacting nations with Christ's gospel.

"What Christ's power and love have done for others, can be realized in your life. This book contains the facts of biblical Salvation for you." – LaDonna & T.L.

Signs, wonders and miracles confirm the ministry of Dr. LaDonna as she promulgates the Gospel in her global crusades.

TRUE CHRISTIANITY involves just two principles. 1) What we *believe* about Christ in our heart. 2) What we *say and do* about our faith.

The mission of every person who follows Jesus Christ is to *be His WITNESS*. That was the passion of early Christians and that is the passion of the true believer today. Peter said, *We are His WITNESSES*. Acs.5:32

# CHAPTER 15

# Embracing Truth

**A**FTER REALIZING the cost of our sins and the price that Jesus paid to redeem us, and after changing our attitude about sin, the Bible alerts us to never attempt to minimize or trivialize or cover them but to confess them openly to God—once and for all, then to trust that they are purged forever.

*Whoever covers their sins shall not prosper: but whoever **confesses** and **forsakes** them shall have mercy.*<sup></sup>Pro.28:13

*If we confess our sins, He is faithful and just to forgive our sins, and to cleanse us from all unrighteousness.*<sup></sup>1Jo.1:9

One needs to take a profound look at one's sins and at their consequences—to search inwardly to be sure that no hidden sins are reserved in one's heart.

This does not mean to grovel in self-denigration about mistakes of the past. It means to identify sins, *once and for all,* and to resolve to abandon and to forsake them, trusting in God's promises that in doing that, our old record is purged forever. Embracing this truth is pivotal for anyone who wants to be BORN AGAIN.

Once sins are identified with true humility in God's presence, then one must never ponder them again, but trust, with total confidence, that *the blood of Jesus Christ, God's Son cleanses from all sins.*[1Jo.1:7]

Once you have realized that your sins are what separated you from God; once you have repented of them and have forsaken them; once you have confessed them to God and have believed that you are saved—BORN AGAIN, then rest absolutely confident that *your sins and iniquities which separated between you and your God* [Isa.59:2] are *removed so far as the east is from the west.* [Psa.103:12] God says, *Their sins and iniquities will I remember no more. Where remission of these is, there is no more offering for sin.*[Heb.10:17-18]

Paul, the apostle said, *Hold to the eternal Life that God has given you, and which you have confessed...before many witnesses.*[1Ti.6:12LB]

*In Jesus Christ we have redemption through His blood the **forgiveness** [**remission**] of sins, according to the riches of His grace.*[Eph.1:7]

◇◇◇

CONFESSION INVOLVES two principle truths in the Christian faith. 1) It means to confess our faith **to Christ**. 2) Then it means to confess our faith **to others** as our witness of Christ. Christianity is 1) Our **believing** in Christ, and 2) our **action** to share Him with others.

The apostle Paul said, *If you confess with your mouth the Lord Jesus, and believe in your heart that God has raised Him from the dead, you shall be saved. Because, **with the heart we believe** in His righteousness* [that is what our *FAITH* is]; *and **with the mouth confession is made** to salvation* [that is what we *SAY AND DO* about our faith]. [Rom.10:9-10]

During forty days after Christ's resurrection, He *showed Himself alive* [Acs.1:3] to His followers, giving proof that the Father had raised Him from the dead. No one would have followed Jesus as a dead prophet.

He told them: *You will receive power after the Holy Ghost comes upon you, and you shall*

121

*be **witnesses** for me...unto the uttermost part of the earth.*<sup>Acs.1:8</sup>

The mission of every person who follows Jesus Christ is to **be His witness**. That was the passion of the early Christians, and that is the passion of true believers today. Peter said, *We are His witnesses.*<sup>Acs.5:32</sup> *Daily in the temple, and in every house, they ceased not to teach and preach Jesus Christ.*<sup>Acs.5:42</sup>

Dr. LaDonna Osborn says, "Christ's passion drove Him to the *Cross*. Now His passion drives us to the *lost*."

That is why the truth of *Confession* is so vital for believers in Christ. The Christian experience of the *new birth* begins by *confessing our sins **to God***. Then the Christian *Life* continues by *confessing our faith **to others***.

❖❖❖

**T**HE UNFATHOMABLE grace of God is doing a profound work in your life right now through the power of the simple but dynamic truths you are pondering.

When you understand and believe these Gospel truths, the *Divine Seeds of Truth* begin to germinate in your life. That is happening while you read these pages.

Now you are ready to embrace the greatest truth in the Bible—and that *Truth* is a PERSON. His name is Jesus Christ. He says, *I am the Way, the TRUTH and the Life.* Joh.14:6

IN RELIGION, sins are confessed over and over, but the sinner is never converted. He or she recommits the same iniquities, seeking again and again forgiveness for the same transgressions. <sup>2Pe.2:22</sup> No *new creature* is engendered. <sup>2Co.5:17</sup> No religion can procreate God's *Divine Life.*

But when one is BORN AGAIN, that person receives the new *Life* of Jesus Christ in the miracle of the *new birth,* and he or she is changed and becomes a child of God! *That is the greatest miracle that any person can experience.*

# CHAPTER 16

# The Greatest Miracle

NOW THAT YOU have acknowledged your sin and have abandoned its self-destructive influence in your life, *the greatest miracle* that anyone can receive from God is taking place in you. By believing these truths, *you are receiving Jesus Christ.* The divine miracle of being BORN AGAIN by the supernatural power of the Holy Spirit is taking place in you as you believe.

The *new birth* is not just a term for joining a Christian religion. Multitudes have done that who have never been *reborn.*

No *religion* can engender in someone the *Life* of God — not even the Christian religion. The Bible says, *Call His name Jesus: for HE shall save His people from their sins.*^Mat.1:23 He saves a person and generates in them His miracle-*Life* when He is received by faith in his word. You can *join* a denomination, but you must be BORN AGAIN to enter the Kingdom of God.

After being BORN AGAIN, it is vital to find a good church to attend. Identifying with a Gospel believing church, one can develop new friends through meeting and fellowshipping with other believers. One can grow in faith and be enriched by the teaching of God's word, and one can share his or her Christian faith for the encouragement of others.

*Joining* a church, in itself, can never engender the *new birth* in someone. (Be sure to read my book THE GOOD LIFE.)

The *new birth* takes place when you receive the new *Life* of Jesus Christ by faith in the teaching of the Gospel.

◇◇◇

JESUS SAID TO Nicodemus, a religious man, *You must be BORN AGAIN.*<sup>Joh.3:7</sup> He added, *Except a person is BORN AGAIN, he* [or she] *cannot see the Kingdom of God.*<sup>Joh.3:3</sup>

Nicodemus was very religious. He was a strict observer of God's law, a proficient teacher of His word and a scrupulous follower of the Old Testament prophets. Although he kept the Sabbath, observed the Ten Commandments, paid his tithes, attended the synagogue and was respected for his good works, Jesus said that he must be BORN AGAIN before he could see God's Kingdom.

This religious man thought Jesus was speaking of a second natural birth. But the Lord said: *That which is born of the flesh is flesh; and that which is born of the Spirit is spirit.* Joh.3:6 The *new birth* is experienced when the *Life* and nature of Jesus Christ are created in a person by a miracle of God's Holy Spirit.

✧✧✧

**F**ROM THE TIME that Adam and Eve sinned against God in the Garden of Eden and were banished from His presence, humanity has been separated from Him by the barrier of their sins. But His immeasurable *Love* impelled Him to find a solution. He offered His Son Who had no sin, as a ransom—as the *propitiation* (atoning sacrifice) for the sins of the world. 1Jo.4:10

Jesus Christ, the innocent one, took upon Himself all of *our* sins 1Pe.2:24 which were then charged to *His* account, 2Co.5:21 and in return, His righteousness was credited to *our* account. He suffered the punishment and endured the judgment that we deserved. He assumed *our* guilt and paid *our* penalty. Isa.53:5-6

He was *the Lamb of God that takes away the sin of the world.* Joh.1:29 *His blood was shed for many for the remission of sins.* Mat.26:28

The Bible says, *The wages of sin is death.* Rom.6:23 Christ died to pay the penalty of *our* sins. That penalty was death. Jesus Christ died on *our* behalf. *We* should have been crucified because we were the ones who had sinned. But He died as *our* substitute.

Since Christ endured the judgment of our sins, *there is therefore now no condemnation to them who are in Christ Jesus.* Rom.8:1

Your debt cannot be paid a second time. Once a debt is paid, it no longer exists. The Bible says, *Where remission is, there is no more offering* [or sacrifice] *for sin.* Heb.10:18

Your sins can never condemn you because your record was purged like a paid debt when Jesus endured *your* judgment on the Cross. You are *saved* when you believe that Christ's death at the Cross redeemed you from spiritual death—from eternal separation from God.

When you stand before God, He will not see your sins because they were *purged* from the record when Christ assumed your guilt and gave His *Life* a ransom for you.

He will only see you and examine you in the light of what His Son did for you at the Cross. He will see the righteousness of Jesus Christ imputed to your account. *God made Him Who knew no sin, to be sin for us; that we might be made the righteousness of God in Christ.*[2Co.5:21]

The 16th Century English Bible says, *Whom God hath set forth to be a propitiation through faith in His blood, to declare His righteousness for the remission of sins that are past, through the forbearance of God.*[Rom. 3:25]

In contemporary English that means that Jesus Christ was offered on the Cross as the atoning sacrifice for all who have faith in Him. Our sins have been *remitted* or *purged* and the righteousness of Christ has been credited to our account; in the records of heaven, we are declared *No longer Guilty!*[Rom. 5:9LB] (The Living Bible says, *God sent Jesus to take the punishment for our sins.*)

◇◇◇

NOW THAT *your* sins have been purged forever like a debt that has been paid; now that you have recognized that Christ ransomed you from the dominion of sin; and now that you have repented and have turned away from sin, you are right now receiving God's new *Life* in you because the wall of separation—the barrier between you and Him no longer exists.

You are receiving His *Life* by believing in His sacrifice at the Cross for *you*. His miracle-*Life* is being engendered in you and you are being BORN AGAIN through the power of the seed-truths that you are embracing in your heart as you read.

Jesus said, *You shall know the truth, and the truth shall make you free.* Joh.8:32 He is coming to **live in you**. He does that because you have resolved to believe in His *Love*, and to receive Him by faith.

This is the *marvel*—the *mystery*—the *miracle* of real salvation. This is not religion; it is the power of the Christ-*Life* transforming you into a new kind of person. Believe it!

The Bible says: *All who receive Him, He gives the power to become the children of God.* Joh.1:12 That is what it means to be BORN AGAIN! You are being BORN AGAIN! The truth about Christ is becoming a reality to you. Your life is conforming to that truth.

In religion, sins are confessed over and over, but the sinner is never converted. He or she recommits the same iniquities, seeking again and again forgiveness for the same transgressions.[2Pe.2:22] No *new creature* is engendered.[2Co.5:17] No religion can procreate God's divine *Life*.

But when one receives the new *Life* of Jesus Christ, that person is BORN AGAIN. He or she is changed and becomes a child of God! **That is the greatest miracle that any person can experience**.

God says, *I will dwell in them, and walk in them; and I will be their God, and they shall be My people...I will be a Father unto you, and ye shall be My sons and daughters, says the Lord Almighty.*[2Co.6:16,18] He is speaking those words to you now. As you believe them, He comes into your life and you are *transformed by the renewing of your mind.*[Rom.12:2]

Jesus said that He and the Father will *come to you, and make their abode with you.*[Joh. 14:23]

That is what it means to be BORN AGAIN. It is a new beginning—not a religion, but a miracle. Be conscious of that miracle. Say

131

"Yes!" to that miracle. By faith, accept the fact of that miracle taking place in you right now.

One can join a Christian church and be baptized, but that never imparts the new *Life* of Christ. It is the miracle of the *new birth* that changes one's nature. *If anyone be in Christ, he* [or she] *is a new creature.*[2Co.5:17] That miracle takes place *by the renewing of one's mind* as one believes the facts of Gospel-redemption.

The infusion of divine *Life* into the human spirit and soul, the procreation or impartation of God's nature into a person is a miracle—a divine mystery. As you believe and embrace these truths, Jesus Christ is coming to you to make His abode with you. You are receiving Him. Your whole nature becomes new. Christ becomes the *Center* of your life—your source of *Life*.

God says, *A new spirit will I put within you.*[Eze.36:26] *A new heart will I give you.*[Jer.31:33] And you are *made perfect in every good work to do His will, working in you that which is well-pleasing in His sight.*[Heb.13:21]

❖❖❖

So IT IS TIME for you to speak the words of this prayer as your positive embrace of Christ and your confession of faith in Him.

When a couple is married, they pledge to accept each other as lifetime partners. By repeating this prayer, you make that pledge to God. So speak these things from your heart:

> Dear Lord, I thank You for sending Jesus to purge me of my sins. I realize that before coming to You, I was condemned by my own sins.
>
> I understand that as Adam and Eve were driven out of Your presence because of their sins, I was separated from You by my sins.
>
> But You sent your Son to assume my guilt and to endure the judgment of my sins so that my debt is paid in full. Now Your word declares me 'Not Guilty!'
>
> So I confess to You my faith that Jesus Christ died for me and shed His blood for the remission of my sins. My old record is purged. You have made me a *new creature*.
>
> With my sins blotted out, nothing now stands between You and me. You are my Father. I am Your child.

I am now reconciled to You by receiving Your divine *Life* in me. You have come to make your abode in my life. I welcome You, Lord Jesus, to live in me from this day forward.

My life is Yours! Your *Life* is mine! Now we have fellowship together. You have put away my sins. You paid my debt. You bore my guilt. You endured my judgment. You shed Your blood and You laid down Your *life* for me.

Your word says, *Behold what manner of love the Father has bestowed upon me, that I should be called a child of God.* 1Jo.3:1

Thank You Lord. *I receive You*, by faith and I believe that You do now *live in me*. I am *saved*—I am BORN AGAIN.

AMEN!

In the Osborn Crusades worldwide, millions of people have learned about Christ and His salvation for the first time, and have received Him into their lives as their Savior and Lord, such as in this Java crusade.

Now you belong to the Family of God. *You are a chosen generation, a royal priesthood, an holy nation, a peculiar people; that you should show forth the praises of Him Who has called you out of darkness into His marvelous light.*
1Pe.2:9

# CHAPTER 17

# Transformation

NOW THAT YOU have received Jesus Christ into your life by faith, a great change has taken place in you. He has granted a new power in you — *miracle*-power *to become a child of God.* Joh.1:12

The Apostle Paul said that when you are in Christ, *old things are passed away; behold, all things are become new.* 2Co.5:17

Being BORN AGAIN, the *Life* of Jesus Christ is miraculously generated in you. As I said before, when you accept Him, He receives you and comes to *make His abode* with you.

Now you belong to the Family of God. Now you are free from the oppressive influence of guilt and condemnation. The Bible says, *He shall save His people from their sins,* Mat.1:21 and *the blood of Jesus Christ cleanses us from all sin.* 1Jo.1:7 Paul adds: *If Christ is **in you**, the body is dead because of sin;*

*but the Spirit is **Life** because of righteousness.*
Rom.8:10

Not only are you purged and forgiven of your sins, you are liberated from sin's domain. *If the Son shall make you free, ye shall be free indeed.* Joh.8:36 *The law of the Spirit of Life in Christ Jesus makes you free from the law of sin and death.*Rom.8:2 *You were the servants of sin [but] being made free from sin, you became the servants of righteousness.* Rom.6:17-18

Paul asks: *How shall we that are dead to sin, live any longer in sin?* Rom.6:2 *Our old person [or nature] was crucified with Christ, so that the body of sin might be destroyed, and therefore we should not serve sin.*Rom.6:6 He counseled: *Reckon yourselves dead to sin* Rom.6:11 [and] *sin shall not have dominion over you.*Rom.6:14

The apostle John says, *Whoever is born of God overcomes the world,*1Jo.5:4 and *does not commit sin.*1Jo.3:8-9 The result is: *That wicked one does not touch him* [or her]. 1Jo.5:18

◇◇◇

THE NEW BIRTH is the spiritual transformation of a person who believes the Gospel and who, by faith in God, receives Jesus Christ into his or her life and resolves to become His follower.

The *new birth* is truly a miracle.

✓ You have become a child of God. Joh.1:12

✓ Your flesh, with its affections and lusts, has been crucified with Christ. Gal.5:24

✓ Your sins are blotted out. Acs.3:19

✓ You are washed from your sins, sanctified and justified. 1Co.6:9-11; Rev.1:5

✓ You have turned from darkness to light; from the power of Satan to the power of God. Acs.26:18; Col.1:13

✓ The old laws and ordinances which you could never measure up to are nailed to the cross. Col.2:14

✓ You have an abundance of new *Life*. Joh. 10:10; 1Jo.5:12

✓ You have full salvation. Rom.1:16; 2Th.2:13

✓ You are recreated in righteousness and true holiness. Eph.4:24

✓ You are a new creature in Christ Jesus. 2Co.5:17

✓ You are a child of light—not of darkness. Eph.5:8

✓ You have redemption through the blood of Jesus and the forgiveness of sins. Eph. 1:7

✓ You are Christ's ambassador now.[2Co. 5:20]

✓ You are God's Elect, His chosen one, and you now have an incorruptible inheritance; you will live in a constant state of blessing and of abundant mercy. [1Pe.1:2-4]

✓ You have Christ's own wisdom, righteousness, sanctification and redemption that is now bequeathed to you.[1Co. 1:30; 2Co.5:21]

✓ You have all of Christ's riches and He has taken away your poverty. [2Co.8:9]

✓ You have His constant presence with you, [Mat.28:20] and Christ has actually come into your life to live and to walk in you. [2Co.6:16]

As His new representative, now you have become a good witness of His *Love*, both in your home and in you community, to *show forth the praises of Him Who has called you out of darkness* [1Pe.2:9] so that *others may see your good works and glorify God.*[1Pe.2:12]

From this day, your will, your emotions, your influence, your energies and your talents will be influenced by His divine *Life*. Your life will be enriched and blessed as you seek to please Him in all that you think and say and do.

Your life is now dedicated to the extension of God's kingdom and for the salvation of hurting people. You have not only received Christ but you have given Him control of your life. **You are transformed.** He is your Lord and you are His child.

Biblical faith means that we expect God to do what He promised. That is why *Faith comes by hearing…the Word of God.* Rom.10:17

Biblical faith means that we embrace His promises and that we share them with others.

Biblical faith means: 1) To *confess our sins to God, believing on Jesus Christ as Lord and Savior,* then it means 2) To *confess Christ to others* who have not yet experienced the *new birth.*

# CHAPTER 18

# Biblical Faith

THE FATHER OF a girl who had died, Mar.5:36 and the father of a demon possessed lad Mar.9:23 came to Christ with their plea for His help. To both of them, He spoke the pivotal truth in being BORN AGAIN; He said: *"Only believe."* Both the lad and the lass were miraculously healed.

The greatest miracle that one can receive from God is the *new birth* and that can only come to a person through *believing*. No religion and no ritual can produce this marvel of God's grace.

The Bible says, *by grace are you saved, through faith.*Eph.2:8 Grace is God's immeasurable *Love* that saves us. *Faith* is the **channel** through which His grace is received. Grace makes God's gift of *Life* available. Faith accepts that gift of *Life*.

The Bible says, **Believe** on the Lord Jesus Christ, and you shall be saved.Acs.16:31

As already quoted, *As many as receive Him, to them He gives power to become the sons* [and daughters] *of God, even to them that **believe** on His name.* Joh.1:12

*By Him, all that **believe** are justified.* Acs.13:39

*Being justified by **faith**, we have peace with God through our Lord Jesus Christ.* Rom.5:1

*We are not of those who draw back unto perdition; but of them that **believe** to the saving of the soul.* Heb.10:30

◇◇◇

**I** HAVE WITNESSED the futility of non-Christian religions around the world. Their adherents are never converted. Their sins are never purged. They return again and again, bringing more offerings or sacrifices, performing more acts of penance in their vain quest for forgiveness and peace.

No human merit and no religious ritual can earn reconciliation with God. It was sin that separated us from Him. To redeem us and to justify us before Him, He gave His Son to ransom us from sin's domain and to redeem us to Himself.

When, through His death on the Cross, Christ purged us from our sins, God's own divine *Life* could then be engendered in us so that we could be part of His Royal Family. We call that experience *Salvation*. All that God asks of us is to *only believe*.

I have said it before in this book, but it bears repeating: No religious ceremony or ritual can engender in a person the miracle *Life* of God. Religious rites, dogmas and creeds are empty and meaningless if one does not have *faith* in the sacrifice of Jesus who endured the judgment of our sins. He laid down His *Life* to pay for our sins and that made possible our *new birth*.

One may recognize one's sins, abhor them and be repentant; one may ask for forgiveness, perform all kinds of penance and make repeated consecrations or sacrifices in search of peace with God. But unless one has *faith* in Christ's sacrificial death on the Cross for the remission of sins, one cannot be BORN AGAIN.

*Biblical Faith* is believing what the Bible says. It is *being fully persuaded that, what God has promised, He is able also to perform.*Rom.4:21

God says, *I am the Lord: I will speak and the word that I shall speak shall come to pass...I will say the word, and will perform it.* Eze.12:25

Jesus said, *Heaven and earth shall pass away, but My words shall not pass away.* Mat.24:34

Putting our trust in the promises of God is *Biblical Faith*. God never fails to honor that faith. *Without faith it is impossible to please God: for whoever comes to Him must* **believe** *that He IS, and that He is a rewarder of them that diligently seek Him.* <sup>Heb.11:6</sup>

**T**HE MIRACLE OF the *new birth* must be accepted by *faith*.

Simple *Biblical Faith* is pivotal to each person who wants to receive Jesus Christ and become His follower.

✓ *Faith* is believing that what God said is true. It means that you expect Him to do what He promised to do. That is why, as we quoted earlier,

✓ *Faith comes by hearing…the Word of God.* Rom.10:17

✓ *Faith* is accepting God's promises and being so convinced of their truth that one acts upon them despite any voice or circumstance that contradicts His word.

✓ *Faith* is believing the Gospel. What is the Gospel? It is the Good News of what Jesus accomplished for us through His death on the cross.

146

✓ *Faith* means that we believe what the Bible says about Christ's substitutionary sacrifice [1Co.15:1-4] whether it seems credible or not.

The Bible makes statements which may appear to be incredible, but Jesus said to *have faith in God.* [Mar.11:22] Following are some of those statements that one cannot humanly rationalize.

◇◇◇

**T**HE BIBLE SAYS *He was wounded for **our** transgressions, He was bruised for our iniquities.* [Isa.53:5] *Who His own self bare **our** sins in His own body on the tree, that we, being dead to sins, should live unto righteousness.* [1Pe.2:24]

*For God made Him [Jesus] Who knew no sin to be sin for **us**…that **we** might be made the righteousness of God in Him.* [2Co.5:21]

It seems irrational to believe that the guilt and judgment of our sins could have been endured, in our name, over two thousand years before we committed them.

That may be why the Gospel is called a *mystery* [Col.1:26-27] and *foolishness.* Paul, the apostle said, *For the preaching of the cross is to them that perish **foolishness**; but to us who are saved, it is the power of God.* [1Co.1:18]

The testimony of millions of people through many centuries give abundant witness that when they have believed on Christ, they have been BORN AGAIN and have discovered peace and a new beginning with God.

Why did God send His Son to ransom us from the power of Satan and of sin? Because of His *grace*. He loved us even though we had broken His law that declares: *The soul that sins, it shall die;* [Eze.18:20] and *The wages of sin is death.* [Rom.6:23]

How did this dilemma of separation from God befall the human race?

✧✧✧

IN THE BEGINNING, Adam and Eve were created perfect, sinless, healthy, pure and happy. They lived in a garden of plenty. They walked and talked with God and had no sense of guilt or fear, of condemnation or of inferiority. [Gen.1:26-31]

Then Satan tempted them to disobey God's word. They ate the fruit that God had forbidden them to eat. [Gen.3:1-6] That was the original sin—*not believing the word of God.* Justice required that sin be punished.
[Rom.6:23]

The consequences of that original sin affected all succeeding generations. *As by one person sin entered into the world, and death by sin; so death passed upon all people, because all have sinned.*[Rom.5:12]

Adam and Eve could no longer live in God's presence in the Garden of Eden. They and their descendants would live forever separated from Him, as slaves of Satan, reaping the harvest of destruction, deterioration and death — the works of the devil — the consequence of sin.

God's law requires that all who sin must die and that law cannot be mitigated. But the Bible says, *He has no pleasure in the death of one who dies.* [Eze.18:32;33:11] *God was not willing that any should perish, but that all should come to repentance.*[2Pe.3:9] So what did He do?

*Love* found a way to honor God's law, yet to ransom humanity from its penalty. Satan, the enemy of humankind, never dreamed that God would pay such a price to redeem those created in His own image.

*God so loved the world that He gave His only begotten Son, that whoever believes in Him should not perish but have everlasting life.*[Joh. 3:16]

God sent His Son to our world where he lived as a man, without sin. Being without sin, He could become our substitute and suffer the penalty of *our* sins.

We could not pay for our own sins, and live, because the penalty of sin is death, and all had sinned, so all were condemned to die. That is why Jesus came. He had not sinned so, because of His *love*, He could suffer *our* judgment in our place.

Jesus was not born of human seed. A divine seed of divine *Life* was implanted in the womb of the Virgin Mary Luk.1:28-32;1:35 by a miracle of the Holy Ghost.

Since the blood comes from the father's seed, Jesus was of divine Lineage—the progeny of God.

The *Life* of Jesus was divine—He was God in the flesh! *The Word was God.* Joh.1:1 The Word *became flesh and dwelt among us.* Joh.1:14 An Old Testament prophet said: *Call His Name Emmanuel, which being interpreted is,* **God with us.** Mat.1:23

That is why John pointed to Him and said: *Behold the Lamb of God that takes away the sins of the world.* Joh.1:29

When He was condemned and crucified, He died as **our** substitute. He took **our** place, enduring the judgment of **our** sins. God's own Son *gave Himself a ransom for **all**.* 1Ti.2:6

God said, *I have given the blood to you upon the altar to make atonement for your souls: for it is the **blood** that makes an atonement for the soul.* Lev.17:11

Jesus said, *This is my blood of the New Testament, which is shed for many for the **remission** of sins.* Mat.26:28

Isaiah said, *The Lord laid on Him* [Jesus] *the iniquity of **us all**,* Isa.53:6 and *for the transgression of my people was He stricken.* Isa.53:8 The prophet added: *His soul was made an offering for sin* Isa.53:10 and Isa.53:11 *He bore the sin of many.* Isa.53:12 That includes the sins that both you and I had committed.

It sounds incredible that Christ could have endured the judgment of **our** sins over two thousand years before we committed them, but this is *the Gospel which* [is] *preached to you...by which you are **saved**,* 1Co.15:1-2 when you embrace it and believe it.

Paul said, *The world by wisdom knew not God, but it pleased God by the foolishness of preaching to save them that believe.* 1Co.1:21 *We preach Christ crucified* [which seems] *a stumbling block, or foolishness.* 1Co.1:23

◇◇◇

YOU MAY NOT understand the north and south poles; you have never seen them. But you accept them and you have faith in their magnetic power. If you ever traveled by plane or crossed the sea by ship, those invisible and mysterious poles guided you to your destination.

You probably do not understand electricity or exactly how your radio, telephone, television or computer functions, but you use them. They work for you. You rely on them.

In the same way, you can *trust* the Good News of Jesus Christ and believe that He took **your** place, suffering the judgment and the penalty of **your** sins.

As He died on the Cross, He uttered the words, *It is finished.* [Joh.19:30] The judgment of **our** sins was suffered by Him and our record was purged. He paid **our** penalty in full.

Remember that no debt can be legally paid the second time. When it is paid **once**, that debt no longer exists. The Bible says, *The wages of sin is death.*[Rom.6:23] then it says, *Christ died for our sins.*[1Co.15:3] Our penalty cannot be suffered or paid twice. Our guilt and our sins cannot legally condemn us again. Salvation is God's gift to all who have faith in His *Love*.

When you believe the Gospel, it means that you have faith in what Jesus accomplished for you in His death on the Cross. You believe that He bore the judgment and paid the penalty of all of your sins and, therefore, they can never condemn you again.

That is why Paul said: *There is therefore now no condemnation to them which are in Christ Jesus.*Rom.8:1

THE PIVOTAL FACTOR in being BORN AGAIN is: Believe the Gospel message— Have faith in what the Bible says that Jesus did for you. What does it really mean to believe the Gospel? The reality and the proof of believing is expressed in one simple word—*Trust*.

I say here what I say to thousands who accept Christ in our crusades all over the world:

✓ *Trust* the Gospel of Jesus Christ and its record of what He did for you. Commit yourself to the fact that you are saved because of what He did.

✓ *Trust* that He suffered enough for you to pay for all of the sins that you have committed or inherited. Christ suffered enough to redeem you, to ransom you out of the hand of *the thief* [who] *comes to steal, and to kill, and to destroy.* Joh.10:10

✓ *Trust* that Christ was perfect; that His blood was sinless.

✓ *Trust* that He had no sin, so He could take your place as your substitute and endure the judgment of your sins.

✓ *Trust* that His blood was efficacious to wash away every sin of yours.

✓ *Trust* that nothing else needs to be done, no further price needs to be paid, no further penalty needs to be suffered, no good works or offerings or sacrifices or penance need to be added to what Christ has already done to redeem you.

✓ *Trust* that He did enough. Rest your soul forever on what the Bible says that Jesus did for you.

Once you have heard and believed the Good News; once you have recognized your sins and repented of them; once you have confessed them and have turned your back on them; once you have come to God as a sinner and have asked His pardon; once you have accepted Jesus Christ into your heart by faith and have resolved to follow Him, then **trust** Him.

Never again do anything or make any sacrifice or perform any ritual or pay any price or take any other step in order to be saved.

✓ *Trust* Jesus Christ.

✓ *Trust* that His sacrifice was sufficient. No religious act that you might perform can add any virtue or merit to your standing before God.

✓ *Trust* that He fully paid *your* debt.

✓ *Trust* that He suffered enough to redeem you from all of your sins and from all of the power of Satan who is your enemy.

✓ *Trust* His payment for your sins. Your offerings and good works cannot improve your state of salvation. They can add nothing to the fact of your redemption.

✓ *Trust* the blood of God's Son.

✓ *Trust* in His *Love* that has been revealed to you, and in His grace that has saved you and redeemed you.

✓ *Trust* in the merits of what Jesus Christ did at the Cross, in *your* place and in *your* name. *It is finished!* [Joh.19:30] Your salvation, your redemption is **fact**. *ONLY BELIEVE.* [Mar.5:36; Joh.9:38;11:27;14:1,10-11;19:35; 20:31; Acs.8:37;13:39;16:31; Rom.10:9-10]

**W**HEN YOU REACH your last day in this life and know you will soon draw your last breath, in that moment continue to **trust** the merits of what Christ accomplished in His death on the Cross, for your salvation.

Do not attempt to think or to say or do anything to improve your salvation at that hour — no ceremony, no ritual, no absolution, no sacrament — nothing. What Jesus did over 2000 years ago was enough. Trust Him and you will be saved. That is what the Bible means by **faith**.

As long as we try to improve our salvation by good works, offerings, rituals, suffering, penance or by any other thought or deed, we are not believing the Gospel — we are not trusting in what Christ did for us.

When I ponder the crowning moment of my life as I will stand before God, no thought or deed will be worthy of any merit before Him Who sacrificed His only Son to redeem me.[Isa.64:6; Jer.2:22; Psa.49:6-15]

I shall plead only what Jesus accomplished for me on the Cross remembering that He was perfect and that He died in my place; that *I have been justified freely by God's grace through the redemption that is in Christ Jesus; Whom He has set forth to be a propitiation through faith in His blood, to declare His righteousness for the remission of* [my] *sins.*
Rom. 3:24-25

✧✧✧

GOD'S WORD makes it clear that the righteousness of Jesus Christ is put to our account when we put our trust in Him. *Whoever does not count on good works, but **believes** on Him Who justifies the ungodly, that one's faith is counted for righteousness.* [Rom.4:5; Heb.9:12,14;10:19-22]

The LIVING BIBLE says, *For God took the sinless Christ and poured into him our sins. Then, in exchange, He poured God's goodness into us!*
2Co.5:21LB

When God examines me, He will see only the *Life* and the righteousness of His own Son that have been attributed to my account since the day that I put my trust in the Gospel. When I ponder that fact, I am calm. I am secure. I have no fear. I am at peace. I believe that He did **enough**. That is **faith**.

*Believe* on the Lord Jesus Christ, and you shalt be saved.[Acs.16:31] The apostle Paul said, *No one can earn the right to heaven by the good things done. No, for being saved is a gift; if a person could earn it by being good, then it wouldn't be a gift... For God declares sinners to be [righteous] in His sight if they have **faith** in Christ to save them.*[Rom.4:4-5LB]

◇◇◇

So, RIGHT NOW, let this prayer be your strong confession of *Biblical Faith*, expressed with all sincerity:

**Dear Lord, I do believe that in Your great mercy, You gave Your Son, Jesus Christ, to ransom me from the slavery and the dominion of sin.**

**I believe that You died in *my* place, as *my* substitute; that You suffered the penalty of *my* sins and that You paid to redeem me so that my record could**

be purged forever, leaving no trace of sin to ever condemn me again.

Even though I was separated from You by my iniquities, <sup>Isa.59:2</sup> You saw me in my fallen state and, because You loved me, You gave Your Son to ransom me out of the dominion of the Destroyer.

Lord Jesus, I thank You for enduring the judgment of *my* sins. When you suffered *my* penalty, *I* was freed. Now, no sin remains to condemn me and I am no longer guilty before God. I can never be judged or sentenced for the sins that You died to redeem me from. They are purged from *my* record.

All of *my* sins were put to *Your* account. All of *Your* righteousness was put to *my* account so that *I* am redeemed and saved.

Now that I am a new creature with the divine *Life* of Jesus Christ, my mission is to share this Good News with others. I have confessed my sins to You. Now I will confess You to others. You were not ashamed to die for me publicly—on the cross. I will not be ashamed to tell of Your *Love* in my world.

In Your vicarious death on the Cross, You did enough for me; there can never be any further price for me to pay. And your sacrifice was not for me alone, but for the whole world. My mission therefore, as Your follower, is to make that Good News known to those who have not been *reborn*. What an honor to be an ambassador of Your *Love*.

From this day I trust in what You did for me at the Cross. Now You can trust me to make that know in my world. I am saved because of what You did for me. You did the same for millions of others so my mission is to tell them. I have Your *Life* now. I am saved now. I dedicate myself to the glorious mission that You gave me when I became Your follower—the mission *to be YOUR WITNESS*.

From this moment I shall do my best to follow You and to share this Good News with others so that they can also receive Your *Life*.

Thank You, Lord, for salvation. I am now a new creature in Christ. I have been BORN AGAIN.

**AMEN!**

God created man and woman *"in His own image,"* as His friends and partners in life. His creation was never made for mediocrity, insignificance, disease, poverty or guilt.

From the breathtaking grandeur of mountain peaks to the fabulous rich valleys of our planet, God placed humanity amidst a rich world of good things for their usefulness, beauty and pleasure.

He said: *"Instead of shame and dishonor, you shall have a double portion of...everlasting joy, and you shall realize that you are a people God has blessed."* Isa.61:7,9 Living Bible

*"If you want a happy, good life,...trust yourself to Christ your Lord."* 1Pe.3:10,15 Living Bible

*"No good thing will He withhold from them that walk uprightly before Him."* Psa.84:11

IF YOU EVER question your salvation, review these chapters. Familiarize yourself with the verses of Scripture in this book, and guard them in your heart.

The Bible says: *They overcame [the adversary] by the BLOOD of the Lamb, and by the WORD of their testimony.* Rev.12:11

# CHAPTER 19

# Now You are Born Again

NOW YOU have been BORN AGAIN through faith in the *Life* of Jesus Christ that has been infused into you through your faith in Him. It has been made possible by the grace of God.

The Lord has come to live in you. Remember that He said, *If you love me, you will keep my words: and my Father will love you, and we will come to you, and make our **abode** with you.* Joh.14:23

You now have His new kind of *Life*. That is the greatest gift that any person can receive from God.

The judgment of your sins has been meted out at the Cross where Jesus suffered your penalty in your place. Those sins can never condemn you again. As we have said before, they are gone—like a debt that **no longer exists** after it has been fully paid.

If you ever question your salvation, review these chapters. Familiarize yourself with the verses of Scripture in this book, and guard them in your heart.

◇◇◇

ONCE YOU have been BORN AGAIN, you have embarked on a new kind of lifestyle. You will be motivated to develop new habits, new acquaintances, new routines, new aspirations. You will want to meet new friends who share the same joy of being saved. You will want to express your thanks to God who has given you this new gift of *Life*. You will want to share your new faith and to be a part of helping spread faith in Christ to your world.

You will begin to think about how you can influence others to know the Lord and to receive His new kind of *Life*. You will want fellowship with other believers. You will want to learn more of the Bible in order to strengthen your faith.

God's *Love* in your heart will yearn for expression, and you will discover that you can only love Him by loving people; that you can only serve Him by serving people; that you can only exalt Him by lifting people.

New dreams, new concepts, new values, new aspirations; new friends, new habits, new relationships will begin to take shape in your life. How does one discover and cultivate these new factors of this new *Life?*

The answer is: *The Church of Jesus Christ.*

The word CHURCH, in biblical terms refers to *the ones who are called out of sin to follow Christ.* They are known as CHRISTIANS. We also call them BELIEVERS.

Jesus said, *Upon this rock I will build My Church and the gates of hell shall not prevail against it.* Mat.16:18 The rock that Jesus spoke about is FAITH—faith that He is *the Christ, the Son of the living God.* Mat.16:16

When you are BORN AGAIN, you become one of those who have been called by Him. The Bible says, *He has saved you and **called you with a holy calling**, not according to your works, but according to His own purpose and grace, which was given to you in Christ Jesus...* 2Ti.1:9

Now, the most important thing for you to do is to begin to find people who have been reborn and who, like you, are among those whom God has *called out of darkness into His marvelous light.* [1Pe.2:9] You will find great encouragement among them, and you will discover many ways in which fellowship with other believers will be of infinite benefit both to you and to them.

People are created by God to be social beings. We need each other. The CHURCH is the institution that Christ Himself has established so that His followers can have rapport with each other and can network together for mutual benefit, pleasure, growth and service.

Believers in Christ form fellowships that greatly enhance their lives. Without this rapport with other believes, one may tend to withdraw, to lose heart, to become diverted, to become weak in faith, or even to drift away from the Lord.

Prayer and Bible study groups facilitate millions of new Christian believers worldwide in discovering and developing meaningful relationships. Such groups are in almost every neighborhood. If you fail to find one, start one where you live. You may be surprised to find how many people in your area have hoped that someone would invite them to have fellowship and to learn about the Lord and His word.

Prayer and Bible groups are formed in offices, homes, among sports teams, golfing professionals, motorcycle clubs, cowboy and Western events, and in almost every conceivable sector of society. Identifying with a group like that, and with a good church, will lead you to new relationships with others who are interested, as you are, in broadening their vista of life.

Paul said, *Let us consider how to stimulate* [how to stir up] *one another to love and good deeds, not forsaking our own assembling together* [not neglecting to meet together]...
Heb.10:24-25NSV/Wm

◇◇◇

IN NATIONS around the world, when people are reborn, one of the vital factors that helps them to grow in their faith and in rapport with others is being part of a good church and Bible class or prayer group where believers get together for fellowship, for prayer, for Bible discussions, and to simply network for building one another's faith, and for finding ways to help others to discover faith in God.

Assembling with other believers is one of our greatest privileges. Believers encourage each other. They strengthen one another by their witness, their faithfulness, their personal ministry to others, their worship to God, their giving for the Lord's work, and in so many other ways.

Christ's CHURCH is where believers pray and worship together, learn from God's word and grow in His grace, give to support the Gospel and have opportunities to witness and share the message of Christ with others in Christian outreaches at home and in missions abroad. The CHURCH is the Family of God. Believers support each other. They minister to each other. They learn from each other. They add strength to each other.

Christ's CHURCH is the place where:

- ✓ A positive attitude and positive faith are fostered in one's life.
- ✓ People are lifted and encouraged.
- ✓ Human hurts are healed.
- ✓ Valuable lessons are learned.
- ✓ Deep and lasting friendships are developed.

✓ Good marriages are made, are repaired, are healed, are strengthened.

✓ Families are bonded and fortified.

✓ Restless and insecure people find peace.

✓ Real Love comes alive.

✓ God and Christian faith are understood.

✓ Jesus Christ becomes Lord.

✓ Life acquires divine purpose and joy.

✓ No one is demeaned, denigrated or disparaged.

✓ *No*bodies become *Some*bodies.

✓ *Every*body discovers their value in life.

The CHURCH of Jesus Christ is God's Royal Family—the Family of Faith, of Hope and of Love. 1Co.13:13

CHRISTIAN LIVING does not promise to be a bed of roses. There will be difficult times. Temptations in this world will put your faith to the test. Billy Graham said, "The devil will *tempt* you, and through that temptation, God will *test* you."

Paul said, *With regard to your former way of life, put off your old self, which is being corrupted by its deceitful desires; and be made new in the attitude of your mind; put on the new self, created to be like God in true righteousness and holiness.* Eph.4:22-24TNIV

You have done that, so now you face a golden future that will be full of His abundant blessings. (Get my book: THE BEST OF LIFE.)

And when problems arise, remember that the Bible says, *No temptation has overtaken you but such as is common to people; God is faithful, Who will not allow you to be tempted beyond what you are able; but with the temptation will provide the way of escape also, that you may be able to endure it.* 1Co.10:13

The Holy Spirit has come to live in you, and He will always empower you to resist the enemy and to overcome evil.

Paul wrote some remarkable advise: *I urge you, by the mercies of God, to present your bodies as living sacrifices, holy and pleasing to God, which is your spiritual act of worship. Do not conform any longer to the pattern of this world, but be transformed by the renewing of your mind. Then you will be able to test and approve what God's will is — His good, pleasing and perfect will.* Rom.12:1-2NIV

Make a practice of learning Bible verses by heart so you can recall them when the enemy tries to divert or tempt or accuse you. David, the Psalmist said to the Lord, *Your word have I hid in my heart, that I might not sin against You.*[Psa.119:11]

Satan is your enemy. When you repent of your life of sin and turn to follow the Lord, the devil will focus every trick possible to confuse you, lie to you, discourage you, accuse you, or tempt you. Why? Because when Christ came into your life, Satan lost his dominion over you.

You will learn that Satan is a liar and an accuser. Jesus said, *He was a murderer from the beginning, and...there is no truth in him. When he speaks a lie, he speaks of his own: for he is a liar, and the father of it.*[Joh.8:44]

You will grow in your faith and discover that when you *resist the devil, he will flee from you;* also that when you *draw near to the Lord, God will draw near to you.*[Jam.4:7-8]

The Bible says of believers in Bible days: *They overcame* [the adversary] *by the **blood** of the Lamb, and by the **Word** of their testimony.*[Rev.12:11] Those two factors are your strongest armor of defense against Satan.

When you are tempted by him, remember that verse: 1) It is through the **blood** of Jesus Christ that you are saved. 2) And it is the

**Word**—the infallible Scriptures which document your salvation. Memorize them and quote them 1) to resist the devil, 2) to confess your faith to God, and 3) to witness of Christ to others.

Remember that God loves you; He cares about you; He is interested in every aspect of your life. Trust Him. Confide in Him. Pray to Him with confidence, like a child talking to its parents. You will realize why Paul said, *We are more than conquerors through Him that loved us.*[Rom.8:37] *If God be for us, who can be against us?* [Rom.8:31] *Thanks be to God, Who gives us the victory through our Lord Jesus Christ.*[1Co.15:57]

◇◇◇

*NOW UNTO HIM that is able to keep you from falling, and to present you faultless before the presence of His glory with exceeding joy, to the only wise God our Savior, be glory and majesty, dominion and power, both now and forever. Amen.* [Jde.24-25]

📖

OSBORN CRUSADES

S. PACIFIC – Surabaya, Indonesia

EUROPE – The Hague, Holland

AFRICA — Uyo, Nigeria

S. AMERICA – Bogota, Colombia

ASIA – Hyderabad, India

HAS THE LORD done something so wonderful for you that you cannot resist telling others about it?

Are His miracles of grace worth sharing with others in our hurting and confused world?

# CHAPTER 20

# New *Lifestyle*

TODAY YOU HAVE embarked upon a new journey. You will discover valuable new relationships that will enrich and enhance your life immeasurably. New friends and new experiences will become a vital part of your daily life.

To insure happiness and success in your new adventure with God and those who follow Him, I offer four dynamic ideas:

✓ *RELATE __TO GOD__ EVERY DAY.*

That is *prayer* – the way you daily talk to God. Mat.7:7-12; Mar.11:23; Joh.14:12-14; Phi.4:6 Talk to Him like you would talk to anyone else. He is your best friend.

✓ *RELATE TO __HIS WORD__ EVERY DAY.*

That is *Bible reading* – the way you allow God to daily talk to you. Mat.4:4; Job.23:12; 1Pe.2:2; 2Ti.3:16-17;2:15 Develop the habit of opening your Bible each day to read some of His Word.

✓ *RELATE TO **SOME BELIEVERS** EVERY DAY.*

That is *Christian fellowship* — the way you daily experience new relationships.<sup>Deu.14:2;</sup> Psa.119:63; Pro.2:20; Ecc.4:9-10; Mal.3:16; Joh.15:15;17:20-21; Acs.2:42; Rom.1:12; 1Co.12:12; 2Co.6:18; Gal.4:6; Eph.2:19; 1Jo. 1:7 You are part of a vital community of believing Christians. In teamwork with them, you discover the joy of learning and the energy of representing Him in our world.

✓ *RELATE TO **NON-BELIEVERS** EVERY DAY.*

That is *Christian witnessing* — the way you daily share Christ with others. Mar.1:17; Luk.19:10; Joh.20:21; Acs.1:8; Eze.3:18; Joh.4:35-36; Mat.9:37-38 Jesus said: *Whoever confesses Me before people, I will confess them before My Father in heaven. But whoever denies Me before people, I will deny them before My Father in heaven.*Mat.10:32-33

Has Jesus Christ done something for you so wonderful that you cannot resist telling others about it? Are His miracles of grace worth sharing in our hurting world? Do people need to know about God's non-judgmental *Love* and His miracle-*Life?*

The purpose and life-mission of each BORN AGAIN person is to be Christ's *witness* to others. The world that surrounds us needs to know that God values each person so much that He gave His Son to redeem them and to bring them back to His side as friends and partners in *Life*.

Without the experience and knowledge of God's *Love*, people have problems without solutions, diseases without cure, fear without peace. They are often unloved, without hope, confused, disheartened, deteriorating in despair. Millions are dead while alive.

Our personal ministry as BORN AGAIN believers is to share with people what has happened to us — what Christ has done in our lives. Begin today to share with your world the Good News of what it means to live in peace with God.

*Know that whoever converts the sinner from the error of his way shall save a soul from death.* Jam.5:20

*Withhold not good from them to whom it is due, when it is in your power to do it.* Pro.3:27

📖

---

I have written three books to help people realize God's blessings in life. 1) YOU ARE GOD'S BEST. 2) THE GOOD LIFE. 3) THE BEST OF LIFE. These books will greatly enrich your own life, and they will reinforce your witness of Christ to others in need of God's nonjudgmental *Love*.

Keep some copies on hand to share with people in your personal ministry. The good seed that you sow will produce a good harvest, and as Jesus said, you will *in no wise lose your reward.* Mat.10:42

# CHAPTER 21

# Decision On Record

**A**S AN ACT OF FAITH, register your decision on the coupon, next page. Receiving Christ as Savior is the greatest miracle you will ever experience and it deserves the distinction of being placed on record.

When you believed the Bible-promises in this book and you prayed and received Christ by faith, an angel recorded your name *in the Lamb's Book of Life.*[Rev.21:27]

Registering your decision on the coupon, next page, will document your personal decision today. If our enemy, the devil, ever causes you to question the validity of your new birth, show him the decision that you place on record today. That is one of the most effective ways that you will learn to *resist the devil, and he will flee from you.* [Jam.4:7]

# MY DECISION

TODAY I HAVE finished reading this book, *"How To Be BORN AGAIN."* I have learned what it means to be *saved*. I have embraced the truths outlined here and I have reverently prayed the prayers included.

BY FAITH IN the Gospel, I have received Jesus Christ as my Savior and Lord. Today, I am BORN AGAIN with the *Life* of Christ. I resolve to do my best to please Him in all that I *think* and *say* and *do*. With His grace and help, I now consider myself as *His witness*, and I shall do my best to share Jesus Christ with others.

RELYING ON HIM to keep me by His grace, I have made this decision and signed this declaration in Jesus' Name.

Signed _____

Date _____

NOW SEAL your decision by writing us a personal letter to further express that you have accepted Jesus Christ, and that you have received the miracle of the *new birth*.

Our faithful co-workers in ministry are joined in faith, praying for every person who reads this book. Our greatest reward is to receive letters from those who have been BORN AGAIN as a result.

We will respond to your letter, and we can become friends and co-workers in sharing the Good News of Christ with others in our hurting world. Perhaps we can send you some special tracts to give to people.

Write us today—lest you forget. Tell us, in your own words, what has taken place in your life. Be sure to let us know the date that you signed this declaration. We are praying for you.

OSBORN International
Box 10, Tulsa, OK 74102 USA
E-mail: OSFO@aol.com
www.osborn.org

# CHAPTER 22

# The Good *Life* is for YOU

**I** HAVE WRITTEN three books to help new believers realize God's *Life*-blessings. 1) YOU ARE GOD'S BEST. 2) THE GOOD LIFE. 3) THE BEST OF LIFE. These books will greatly enrich your own life, and they will reinforce your witness of Christ to those who are in need of God's nonjudgmental *Love*.

I wrote THE GOOD LIFE as a sequel to this book on the *new birth*, and published it as a mini-Bible school for new followers of Christ in the French-speaking world. I did it to help them realize the fullness of God's blessings. Later, we published it in English. Now it is also published in Russian, Polish, Spanish, Bulgarian, Mandarin Chinese, and in many other major languages.

THE GOOD LIFE contains 1,478 Bible references, and is full of discoveries, revealing the secrets of happy, successful Christian living. It concludes with the CHURCH'S eighteen fundamental *Gospel Tenets of Faith*, expressed in terms that are easy to understand and that create a solid base of *Biblical Faith*.

THE GOOD LIFE is a book of divine secrets for happiness, health, success and prosperity. God is your partner and He will lead and bless you with His very **best**.

*Forget not **all** of His benefits.*<sup>Psa.103:2</sup>

*No good thing will God withhold from them that walk uprightly...Blessed is the one who trusts in Him.*<sup>Psa.84:11-12</sup>

THE GOOD LIFE is for you! Believe it!

# CHAPTER 23

# Promises To Treasure

*I*F YOU CONFESS *with your mouth the Lord Jesus, and believe in your heart that God raised Him from the dead, you shall be saved. For with the heart one believes for righteousness; and with the mouth confession is made unto salvation.*Rom.10:9-10

Paul, the apostle said, *I have declared unto you the Gospel which I preached...which you have received, and wherein you stand; By which also you are saved, if you keep in memory what I preached to you, unless you have believed in vain.*

*For I delivered to you...that which I also received, [1] how that Christ died for our sins according to the Scriptures; [2] that He was buried, [3] that He rose again the third day according to the Scriptures: and [4] that He was seen of Cephas, then of the twelve, then of above five hundred at once; of James, then all of the apostles, and of me, [says Paul].*<sup>1Co.15:1-7</sup>

*For I am not ashamed of the Gospel of Christ: for it is the power of God unto Salvation to everyone that believes.*<sup>Rom.1:16</sup>

*All the prophets give witness of Jesus Christ, that through His Name whoever believes in him shall receive remission of sins.*<sup>Acs.10:43</sup>

*Therefore being justified by faith, we have peace with God through our Lord Jesus Christ.*<br>
Rom.5:1

Speaking of the miracles wrought by the Lord during His earthly ministry, John said, *These are written, that you might believe that Jesus is the Christ, the Son of God; and that believing you might have Life through His Name.*<br>
Joh.20:31

*Whoever hears My Words and believes on Him that sent Me, has Everlasting Life, and shall not come into condemnation; but is passed from death unto Life.*<sup>Joh.5:24</sup>

*And this is the record, that God has given to us eternal Life, and this Life is in His Son. And whoever has the Son has Life; and whoever does not have the Son of God does not have Life.*<sup>1Jo.</sup><br>
5:11-12

*For you are the children of God by faith in Jesus Christ.* <sup>Gal.3:26</sup> And you *are kept by the power of God through faith unto salvation.*<sup>1Pe.1:5</sup>

*God's divine power has given to us all things that pertain to Life and godliness…Whereby are given unto us exceeding great and precious promises: that by these you might be partakers of the Divine Nature.*<sup>2Pe.1:4</sup>

*For whoever is born of God overcomes the world: and this is the victory that overcomes the world, even our faith. Who is the one who overcomes the world, but he or she who believes that Jesus is the Son of God?* <sup>1Jo.5:4-5</sup>

*I am come a Light into the world, that whoever believes on Me should not live in darkness.* <sup>Joh.12:46</sup>

*Whoever believes on Me, as the Scripture has said, out of his belly shall flow rivers of living water. (He spoke this of the Spirit, which they that believe on Him should receive.)* <sup>Joh.7:38-39</sup>

*Blessed is she* [or he] *that believed: for there shall be a fulfillment of the things which have been spoken…from the Lord.*<sup>Luk.1:45RV</sup>

*I say to you, all things whatever you pray and ask for, believe that you have received them, and you shall have them.*<sup>Mar.11:24RV</sup>

*Whoever believes on Me, the works that I do shall he* [or she] *do also; and greater works than these shall they do; because I go to My Father, and whatever you shall ask in My Name, that will I do, that the Father may be glorified in the Son.* Joh.14:12-13

*Jesus said, If you can believe, all things are possible to the one who believes.* Mar.9:23

*For I say...to everyone among you...* [that] *God has dealt to each one the measure of faith.* Rom.12:3

**Because** *without faith it is impossible to please Him; for whoever comes to God must believe that He is, and that He is a rewarder of them that diligently seek Him.* Heb.11:6

*Faith comes by hearing, and hearing by the Word of God.* Rom.10:17

*Looking unto Jesus the author and finisher of our faith; Who for the joy that was set before Him endured the cross, despising the shame* [on our behalf], *and is set down at the right hand of the throne of God* Heb.12:2 *where He is now the one Mediator between God and people, the man Christ Jesus; Who gave Himself a ransom for all* 1Ti.2:5-6 *because He will have all people to be saved, and to come to the knowledge of the truth.* 1Ti.2:4

So since *we do not have a high priest that cannot be touched by the feeling of our infirmities; but was in all points tempted like we are, yet without sin, let us therefore come boldly to the Throne of Grace, that we may obtain mercy, and find grace to help in time of need.* Heb.4:15-16

*Ask, and it shall be given you; seek, and you shall find; knock, and it shall be opened unto you...If a child shall ask bread of any of you that is a father, will he give his child a stone? or if the child asks a fish, will he for a fish give the child a serpent?* Luk.11:9-11

*If you then, being evil, know how to give good gifts to your children, how much more shall your Father which is in heaven give good things to them that ask Him?* Mat.7:11

*These things have I written unto you, that you may know that you have eternal Life, even to you that believe on the name of the Son of God.* 1Jo.5:13RV

*ALL SCRIPTURE is given by inspiration of God, and is profitable for doctrine, for reproof, for correction, for instruction in righteousness.* 2Ti.3:16

*Therefore shall you lay up these My Words in your heart and in your soul, and bind them for a sign upon your hand, that they may be as frontlets between your eyes.* Deu.11:18

*Let the Word of Christ dwell in you richly in all wisdom.* Col. 3:16

# CHAPTER 24

# Finding the Answer

**W**HEN YOU question your salvation,
read *1 John 5:11-13; John 3:16*

When you are tempted to sin,
read *James 1:2-4; and 12-15;*
*1 Corinthians 10:13*

When you feel loneliness or depression,
read *Hebrews 13:5-6; Psalms 23.*

When you receive unfair treatment,
read *1 Peter 2:19-23; 1 Peter 4:12-15.*

When you need direction,
read *Proverbs 3:5-6; James 1:5.*

When you need forgiveness,
read *1 John 1:9; Hebrews 4:15-16.*

When you are tired and weary,
read *Matthew 11:28-30; Galatians 6:9.*

When you face a challenge,
read *Philippians 4:13.*

When problems assail you,
  read *Psalms 55:22; 1 Peter 5:7.*

When you need peace in difficult times,
  read *John 14:27; John 16:33;*
    *Philippians. 4:6-7.*

When you are confronted by danger,
  read *Psalms 91; Psalms 121.*

When tempted by selfish motives,
  read *1 John 2:15-17; Psalms 106:13-15;*
    *Philippians 4:8.*

When confronted by sorrow,
  read *John 14:1, 18; 2 Corinthians 1:3-5;*
    *Romans 8:26-28.*

When you need strength,
  read *Ephesians 6:10-13; 2 Timothy 2:1;*
    *Psalms 138:3.*

When you fear that you might fall,
  read *Philippians 1:6; 1 Peter 1:5.*

When you face financial needs,
  read *Psalms 34:10; Philippians 4:19;*
    *3 John 2.*

When you are tempted by impatience,
  read *James 1:2-4; Romans 8:28-29.*

When you are tempted by pride,
  read *Philippians 2:3-8; 1 Corinthians 4:7.*

When your life's purpose needs focus,
  read *Matthew 5:48; Matthew 22:36-40;*
    *Matthew 25:31-40.*

## CHAPTER 25

# A Daily Prayer

NOW CHRIST lives in you. You are His Body. Paul, the apostle said, *For God is at work **within you**, helping you want to obey Him, and then helping you to do what He wants.* Phi.2:13LB

So learn to let Jesus express Himself in and through you as you follow Him.

Make this part of your daily prayer:

HEAVENLY FATHER,
When there is a need for *teaching*,
TEACH through me.
When there is need for *truth*,
SPEAK through me.
When there is a need for *love*,
LOVE through me.
When there is a need for *music*,
SING through me.
When there is a need for *understanding*,
LISTEN through me.

When there is need for *counseling*,
ADVISE through me.
When a *gift* is needed,
GIVE through me.
When a *helping hand* is needed,
REACH and TOUCH through me.
In Jesus' Name I pray this prayer,
AMEN!

We paint our picture of Christ in our world by our thoughts, our words, our *Actions*. We *interpret* Him. He paid to redeem us so He can live in us. Now we express Him. He is our Spirit. We are His flesh. Combined, that is a *Christian*. Our gift in life is to uplift people. That is biblical *Spirituality*. Jesus does His work through us. Our seed procreates, He depends on us. We are *BORN AGAIN* Christians.

For over 50 years I've witnessed that Christ has not changed. He is as relevant today as ever. His passion drove Him to the *cross*. Now it drives believers to the lost. The *World* is the Heart of the Church. The *Church* is the Hope of the World. Our goal: 1) *Establish People in Christ,* then 2) *Establish Christ in people*. This book unveils the reborn *You – Christ's Life and Love in flesh, YOU – a BORN AGAIN Christian.*

THE APOSTLE JOHN wrote a brief Letter to new Christians 1Jo.2:12-14 and we include it here for your growth.

Earlier, John wrote a Gospel, and told us why he wrote it: *That you might believe that Jesus is the Christ, the Son of God; and that believing, you will have Life through His Name.* Joh.20:31

John's Gospel helps you to BELIEVE. Some form of the word, *"believe,"* appears nearly one hundred times.

John's Letter helps you to KNOW certain facts. Some form of the word, *"know,"* appears nearly forty times. He says: 1) We must BELIEVE like Christians, and 2) we must ACT like Christians. In chapters 1-3, Christian LIVING is made clear. In chapters 4-5, Christian BELIEVING is emphasized.

So, as you read John's letter of love and faith, you will grow in your *fellowship* with God and in your *relationship* with people.

# CHAPTER 26

# The Love Letter

## COMPILED FROM
## THE FIRST EPISTLE OF JOHN

*THAT WHICH WE have seen and heard declare we unto you, that you also may have fellowship with us: and truly our fellowship is with the Father, and with His Son Jesus Christ.*

*If we walk in the light, as He is in the light, we have fellowship one with another, and the blood of Jesus Christ His Son cleanses us from all sin.*

*If we say that we have no sin, we deceive ourselves, and the truth is not in us.*

*If we confess our sins, He is faithful and just to forgive us our sins, and to cleanse us from all unrighteousness.*

*And He is the propitiation for our sins: and not for ours only, but also for the sins of the whole world.*

*Love not the world, neither the things that are in the world. If anyone loves the world, the love of the Father is not in that one.*

*For all that is in the world, the lust of the flesh, and the lust of the eyes, and the pride of life, is not of the Father, but is of the world.*

*And the world passes away, and the lust thereof: but the one who does the will of God abides forever.*

*B*EHOLD, WHAT MANNER *of love the Father has bestowed upon us, that we should be called the Children of God: therefore the world does not know us, because it did not know Him.*

*Beloved, now are we the children of God, and it does not yet appear what we shall be: but we know that, when He shall appear, we shall be like Him; for we shall see Him as He is.*

*Whoever commits sin is of the devil; for the devil has sinned from the beginning. For this purpose the Son of God was manifested, that He might destroy the works of the devil.*

*Whoever is born of God does not commit sin; for His seed remains in that one: and he, or she cannot sin, because they are born of God.*

*For THIS IS the message that you heard from the beginning, that we should love one another.*

*We know that we have passed from death unto life, because we love the children of God. Whoever does not love others abides in death.*

*Here is how we perceive the love of God, because He laid down His life for us: and we ought to lay down our lives for others.*

*But whoever has this world's good, and sees his brother [or sister] have need, and shuts up their bowels of compassion from that needy one, how does the love of God dwell in such a person?*

*My little children, let us not love in word, neither in tongue; but in deed and in truth.*

*Let us love one another: for love is of God; and every one that loves is born of God, and knows God.*

*Whoever does not love does not know God; for God is love.*

*In this was manifested the love of God toward us, because that God sent His only begotten Son into the world, that we might live through Him.*

**H**EREIN IS LOVE, *not that we loved God, but that He loved us, and sent His Son to be the propitiation for our sins. If God so loved us, we ought also to love one another. No one has seen God at any time. If we love one another, God dwells in us, and His love is perfected in us.*

*Here is how we know that we dwell in Him, and He in us, because He has given us of His Spirit.*

*There is no fear in love; but perfect love casts out fear: because fear has torment. Whoever fears is not made perfect in love.*

*We love Him, because He first loved us.*

*If a person says, I love God, and hates another person, he* [or she] *is a liar: for anyone who does not love a brother* [or a sister] *whom they have seen, how can they love God Whom they have not seen?*

*And this commandment we have from Him, That anyone who loves God loves also their brother* [or their sister].

*For whatever is born of God overcomes the world: and this is the victory that overcomes the world, even our faith.*

*Whoever has the Son has Life; and whoever does not have the Son of God does not have Life.*

*T*HESE THINGS HAVE I *written to you that believe on the name of the Son of God; that you may know that you have eternal Life, and that you may believe on the name of the Son of God.*

*And this is the confidence that we have in Him, that, if we ask any thing according to His Will* [or His word of promise], *He hears us:*

*And if we know that He hears us, whatever we ask, we know that we have the petitions that we desired of Him.*

**May God Bless You.** We have published this book to help you to be BORN AGAIN, to encourage you in your faith in Christ and to inspire you in your witness of Him to others.

Write and tell us what the Lord has done for you. The three books that I mentioned (*YOU ARE GOD'S BEST*, *THE GOOD LIFE*, and *THE BEST OF LIFE*) will greatly strengthen your faith, and they will reinforce your Christian witness. Keep extra copies on hand to share with others.

OSBORN International
Box 10, Tulsa, OK 74102 USA
E-Mail: OSFO@aol.com
www.osborn.org

## BIBLE-BOOK ABBREVIATIONS
## IN THIS BOOK

| | | | |
|---|---|---|---|
| Gen | Genesis | Rom | Romans |
| Lev | Leviticus | 1Co | I Corinthians |
| Num | Numbers | 2Co | II Corinthians |
| Deu | Deuteronomy | Gal | Galatians |
| Job | Job | Eph | Ephesians |
| Psa | Psalms | Phi | Philippians |
| Pro | Proverbs | Col | Colossians |
| Ecc | Ecclesiastes | 2Th | II Thessalonians |
| Isa | Isaiah | 1Ti | I Timothy |
| Jer | Jeremiah | 2Ti | II Timothy |
| Eze | Ezekiel | Tit | Titus |
| Zep | Zephaniah | Heb | Hebrews |
| Mal | Malachi | Jam | James |
| Mat | Matthew | 1Pe | I Peter |
| Mar | Mark | 2Pe | II Peter |
| Luk | Luke | 1Jo | I John |
| Joh | John | Jde | Jude |
| Acs | Acts | Rev | Revelation |

# Osborn International
# Global Ministry

**T**HE MISSION of Christianity is to witness of Christ to *all the world* , to *every creature.*[Mar.16:15] The Apostle Paul was consumed with this passion.

He said, *Whoever shall call on the name of the Lord shall be saved.*[Rom.10:13]

Then Paul asked the pivotal questions that have motivated the Osborns in each arm of their world ministry:

*How shall they call on him in whom they have not believed? and how shall they believe in him of whom they have not heard? and how shall they hear without a preacher? and how shall they preach except they be sent?* [Rom.10:14-15]

In 1949, OSBORN INTERNATIONAL was instituted **to express and propagate the Gospel of Jesus Christ to all people throughout the world.** Their maxim: **No one deserves to hear the Gospel repeatedly until everyone has heard it once.** Their motto: **One Way—**

*Jesus; One Job—Evangelism.* Their guiding principle: *Every Christian believer—a witness for Christ.*

During almost six decades, they have proclaimed the Gospel to millions in 86 nations. Dr. Daisy Osborn passed away in 1995. Dr. LaDonna, the Osborn daughter, as CEO and Vice-President of OSBORN INTERNATIONAL, is making possible the expansion of ministry in many new fields such as Russia, French-speaking Africa, Eurasia and China.

As a world evangelist, Dr. LaDonna's passion to win souls drives her to the remote corners of the earth. As a pastor, her passion to build Christians into dynamic witnesses for Christ motivates her in teaching the truths of Redemption. As Bishop of over 600 churches and ministry leaders, her passion to help pastors, and evangelists, to grasp God's vision energizes her in apostolic ministry both at home and abroad.

Dr. LaDonna's teaching on Redemption is establishing new believers and training Church leaders in the dynamics of Christ-centered ministry. Her newest book, GOD'S BIG PICTURE, is already published in Russian, Bulgarian, the national Chinese language of Mandarin, and in Portuguese.

Her presentation of the biblical Gospel message through books, audio and video teachings and through her life-changing Bible courses has become the hallmark of her international ministry. She says: *The world is the heart of the Church and the Church is the hope of the world,* adding, *The passion that sent Christ to the cross is the passion that sends us to the lost.*

She contends: *Without the world, the Church is meaningless, and without the Church, the world is hopeless.*

It is her resolve to faithfully proclaim the same *Gospel message* that has been heralded by her brave parents for over a half-century in nearly a hundred nations the world.

As this book goes to press, the OSBORN INTERNATIONAL is approaching its sixth decade. From its inception it has followed the example of Paul's unrelenting quest to bring the light of the Gospel to those in spiritual darkness.

T.L. and Daisy Osborn went to India as missionaries in 1945, but not knowing about miracles, they were unable to convince Moslems and Hindus about Christ. Heartbroken, they returned to the USA realizing that people must have proof of the Gospel and evidence that Jesus is alive. *Jesus of Nazareth was…**approved of God** among people by **miracles** and **wonders** and **signs**, which God did by him in the midst of the people.*[Acs.2:22]

The Lord mercifully guided them through their dilemma. Christ appeared to T.L. Then they discovered biblical truths that build faith for miracles today.

Their ministry of World Evangelism began back in the era of colonial domination of so-called "Third World" nations. In open air campaigns, they addressed audiences of from 20,000 to 300,000 throughout the dangerous years of nationalism and political rejection of foreign domination.

Because of the apostolic example of their ministry in action, and through their books, docu-miracle videos and tons of literature, tens of thousands of national men and women have arisen with fresh faith and have become great Gospel ministers to the unreached. Many of them are among the successful Christian leaders in nations of the world today.

OSBORN INTERNATIONAL has sponsored over 30,000 national preachers as full time missionaries, to their own and neighboring unreached areas, and has sponsored the establishing of new churches in over 100,000 tribes and villages that were previously unchurched.

The OSBORN Gospel literature is published in 132 languages. OSBORN docu-miracle crusade films, audio and video cassettes, and Bible courses for study and for public evangelism, are produced in over seventy major languages.

Huge shipments of soulwinning tools for Gospel missions and for Christian workers have been airlifted and surface-shipped into nations abroad.

Scores of four-wheel drive mobile vehicles have been provided for evangelism worldwide, loaded with films, projectors, screens, generators, public-address systems, audio cassettes and cassette players, plus enormous quantities of literature in one hundred and thirty-two languages.

The OSBORN books have affected millions of lives. Dr. Daisy's five major books are unprecedented in Christian literature **for women**, revealing their identity, dignity, equality and destiny in God's redemptive plan.

In 1951 T.L. wrote his first book, HEALING THE SICK. It has penetrated the world and is now in its enlarged 46th edition. Over a million copies are in print. A unique 512 page documentary, THE GOSPEL ACCORDING TO T.L. & DAISY, is published and is unlike any other publication.

Today, OSBORN INTERNATIONAL is esteemed as a preeminent voice in world missions for this 21st Century. Its programs are making a global impact upon the lives of millions of people.

When dates can be synchronized, Dr. LaDonna and her father, Dr. T.L., minister together in mass miracle crusades and in miracle-*Life* seminars. They share the crusade preaching, the public mass ministry to the sick, and the seminar teaching, bringing new faith, hope, and love—and *Life* to multitudes of people worldwide.

Dr. LaDonna Osborn has become a decisive influence in world missions. Both of her sons are involved in world missions and her two daughters are involved in their home churches. Rev. Donald has ministered in Romania, USA, Bolivia, Chile and Ecuador. Rev. Tommy has conducted great gospel crusades in over forty nations of the world.

The Osborn family is determined that the nations and the peoples of Century 21 will realize 1) that the Bible is valid today, 2) that the mission of each believer is to win the lost to Christ, 3) that every Christian is to be Christ's witness, and 4) that the supernatural is what distinguishes Christianity from the religions of the world.

These issues constitute the essence of the OSBORN INTERNATIONAL ministry. The witness of T.L. and LaDonna is expressed best by the words of John: *We bear record of the Word of God, and of the testimony of Jesus Christ, and of the things that we have seen.* Rev.1:2 *We...testify of these things and have written them: and we know that our testimony is true.* Joh.21:24

### GLOBAL PUBLISHER

OSBORN PUBLICATIONS
P.O. Box 10
Tulsa, OK 74102 USA

✦✦✦

### FRENCH DISTRIBUTOR

ÉDITIONS
MINISTÈRES MULTILINGUES
909, Boul. Roland-Therrien
Longueuil, Québec J4J 4L3, CANADA

✦✦✦

### GERMAN PUBLISHER

SHALOM — VERLAG
Pachlinger Strrasse 10
D-93486 Runding, CHAM, Germany

✦✦✦

### PORTUGUESE PUBLISHER

GRACA EDITORIAL
Caixa Postal 1815
Rio de Janiero–RJ–20001, Brazil

✦✦✦

### SPANISH PUBLISHER

LIBROS DESAFIO, Apdo. 29724
Bogota, Colombia

✦✦✦

*(For Quantity Orders, Request Discount Prices.)*